AF252156

L'élégance De Paris
lelegancedeparis.com

LEGACY OF A HUSTLER

LEGACY OF A HUSTLER

Terry Christoher Carney

Written by
TERRY C. CARNEY

Co-written by
MELINDA B CARNEY

TATE PUBLISHING
AND ENTERPRISES, LLC

Published by Tate Publishing & Enterprises, LLC
127 E. Trade Center Terrace | Mustang, Oklahoma 73064 USA
1.888.361.9473 | www.tatepublishing.com

Tate Publishing is committed to excellence in the publishing industry. The company reflects the philosophy established by the founders, based on Psalm 68:11,
"The Lord gave the word and great was the company of those who published it."

Book design copyright © 2015 by Tate Publishing, LLC. All rights reserved.
Cover design by Maria Louella Mancao
Interior design by Shieldon Alcasid

Published in the United States of America

ISBN: 978-1-68187-400-5
Biography & Autobiography / Personal Memoirs
15.09.09

ACKNOWLEDGMENTS

A VERY SPECIAL thanks to: my Lord and Savior Jesus Christ, my wife, my mother Mary Carney (RIP), my father Howard, my brothers and sisters who are living and on the other side, Butch (RIP), and Mary El (RIP).

My children Bunnie, Opal, Tea Tea, Marcus, Geno, Brittany, Lawon; my grandson Jeremiah Francisco; my granddaughters Aryah, Alyah, and Niliah.

My big brother Batman, his wife Karen (RIP), Big Poppa (RIP), Dr. Joseph Jennings (RIP), Ice T, Sean E. Sean, 6-9 East Coast, Jawbone, my Latin Kings family, my East Coast 6900, Lisa Ling, Liz Lo, Amy Bucher and Part2 Pictures; Oprah Winfrey, the O. WN network, Tyler Perry, Magic Johnson, Carson Daley, and the employees at the city of Beverly Hills.

Special thanks to my baby boy's girlfriend Brandi Hassell and Lil D a.k.a. Darian. My son-in-law Lil Lo Lo and my son Tea Tea's girlfriend Kelsea. And a special thanks to my son, Briley, stay strong and keep ten toes to the flo and your back against the wall. Don't trust nothing moving but God. Do your time then come back home, son, and get it together. RIP to my big brother Bruce RIP; Flora

Hunter, my boy Big Daddy Buck's mom. I miss you bro and I love you. RIP to Ed Slade and Bertha Savoid, I miss you guys and I love you both. Special thanks to William Acks, Liz Lo, Eric Strauss; my lil cuzzin, the undefeated boxing champion, keep it poppin' Lydell Rhodes, your father would be so proud of you. And peace and one love to my lil cuzzin Matt Kemp bro. I hate that you're not a Dodger anymore but the Padres are all good keep getting your money, my man, that's what's up and keep rippin' our turf 41st Street and Greenwood. Tell Stink, Thurman, Debbie, and Katie, and your pops Glen that I said, "What's up? We're doing the damn thing." And I would like to say "What's up" to my lil brother Antione Cason, much love to you, brother. I will always love you for all that you have done and continue to do for your lil brother, Lawon Darion Carney, you and Darren Sproles, I have nothing but mad love for you both. I will continue to pray for you while you both continue your careers in the NFL, and thank you both so much, and one love guys. RIP to my big brother Bruce, I miss you bro and I love you.

Special thanks to the city of Beverly Hills, California, and everyone that works for the city. Special thanks to my mentor George Chavez, the director of public works. And my boys Robert Martell and Eugene, and my boy Hosea from waste water and everyone that works for public works in Beverly Hills, California. And my whole street team of Beverly Hills: Frank Victoria, Tommy Padilla, Paul

Neria, Tyrone Barton, Robert, Eugene, Juan, Kevin, Javier, Edwardo, Fidencio, love all you guys and everyone else on the bottom floor of public works. It's too many of you to name, so you all know that I'm riding for all y'all! My son Briley Lambert, stay strong and stay alive and come home out of that cage one love.

Contents

1

THE BACKGROUND

I WAS BORN in the late sixties in Denver, Colorado, to proud parents, Howard and Mary Carney. I had fourteen living brothers and sisters at the time of my arrival; my birth name is Terry Christopher Carney. My middle name, Christopher, was given to me after my mother's father whom she confessed she never really knew.

In truth, I often wondered why my mother named me after a man who was labeled a "trick daddy." It's what they called men back in the day who didn't have time for their children because they were too busy wining and dining whore's. My mother would tell me stories about her father who brought his fancy whore's around her and her two sisters, popping in and out of their lives maybe once every two or three years. He laced his women with the finest clothes and jewels. My mother and aunts, they were just happy to see him whenever they could, just like that old saying "You have to love what you have."

They loved him unselfishly, but my grandfather was so ill that when his baby girls ran to him and his whore's for hugs, desiring to be held and cuddled, he pushed them away. He literally made them stay back because he did not want them to touch or dirty he and his whore's clothes and beautiful jewelry.

After hearing these stories from my mother and finally meeting him and getting to know him in his golden years, we became very close and really loved each other. But I still couldn't help thinking that back then, for him to be so cruel to his own flesh and blood daughters. He was just screwed up in the head. To this day, I don't know why I had to be the one to continue to carry his name. But I guess my mother just wanted to have one son to remember him by.

She loved her father so much and was loyal to him up until his dying day. Even after the hard life and emotional scars, she endured behind his neglect and abuse. My mother's mother died at a very young age, leaving her to raise herself and her two sisters at ten years old during the Great Depression. How they survived it, only God knows. I guess you can say somebody up there really had their hands on them. Up until the day she passed over to heaven, she was still the most loving, kind, and purehearted woman I had ever known. She was always there for me and was the one lady that I could count on.

I can't tell the lie that you hear others hollering about like, "My father wasn't around!" or "My mother was a crackhead!" You see, I was blessed with two of the most honest and hardworking parents that most kids would kill for.

My father is an upstanding, honest man. In my own words, he is the closest man to Jesus that I know in this world. You could not pay him to do anything wrong. My father is so straight-that he wouldn't keep money from a bank if they accidentally overcounted his money. It could be a quarter or more and he would bring it back. My father is the only man I know who could receive a call at three in the morning; rain, sleet or snow, he would get up to help that person on the other end of the phone line no matter who it was. Even if it was way across town, he would be there to help. You better believe they'd get the lecture of their lives. One thing everyone I grew up with knew that they could count on Mr. C, and they called on him for all those reasons.

Every kid in the neighborhood called my mother "Mama" because that's just who she was, and they called my dad Mr. C.

My mama created a community center so that we'd all have some place to go after school and during the summer break since no one else in the community seemed to care about the kids in our hood. They surely never tried to lend a helping hand, and this was to keep their own kids entertained. When they got tired of looking at them, they sent them to the community center. You couldn't get them to do for their own. That's just how it was, so instead of them going to their parents with their problems, they came to my mother for advice. My mother was like the black Dear Abby; only she wouldn't answer back with just a letter. She actually walked them through their problems; hugged and gave them the love they needed, just like a mother should. This is why my mother became "Mama" to over fifty hood kids and still is to this day. She treated them like they were her flesh-and-blood children. Whatever she did for us, she did for them. That is just how it was.

Our house was the place where everyone hung out, no matter where we moved to. My father worked sixteen hours a day in construction, and my mother worked up to ten hours daily running the community center. Her job was more like twenty-four hours because kids followed her home and tended to stay at our house. Although both my parents worked for our family to survive, we still hovered a little above water on a monthly basis, putting us on the low income scale. The fact that my brothers and I were nothing but trouble didn't help the situation.

You see it doesn't matter how good your parents are. They could be the best like my parents and try to teach you morals and honest values. We were taught to work hard for what we wanted in order to succeed, but we made our own definition of those positive life lessons that our parents raised us to follow. With all this support and positive upbringing, you wonder how kids go astray. The truth is that no matter how you raise your kids, you can give them the world, but you can also lose them.

Without the proper communication, you won't see it. You need someone with the vision to see where your kids are. Someone that just has that gift and has been there and acknowledges it before it gets too far out of hand. It's just that simple. Growing up in my household with so many kids around made it extremely difficult for my mom and dad to stay on top of each and everyone of us and guide us properly. Especially with boys, you have to stay on top of them 24/7 because we are all so hardheaded and sneaky. You may say that your baby will never do anything like the stories you are about to read. Denial and blindness will make your son first to get caught up in the game. By keeping that frame of mind, he is already one step ahead of you and knows it. He is going to keep you in the dark until you visit him at his grave site or the correctional center. I know this from real life experience.

The hardest thing I have gone through alongside my mother is knowing that some fools killed my brother; there is no pain like a mother having to bury a child or watching a mother's reaction when a judge drops his gavel.

The uncertainty of not knowing whether she will ever see her child again or if he'll survive his bid. Witnessing one of your children getting time hurts like the first time, every time. I have seen my mother being destroyed by this, and it just felt like it was me seeing it through her own eyes, always knowing there wasn't a thing I could do about it. Beyond everything I have gotten myself into, this was the hardest to deal with. Out of fifteen kids even with good parents like ours, nine boys out of ten walked astray and gave my parents the blues. All of our problems started in my hometown in Denver, Colorado, after I was born.

2

AND DON'T COME BACK!

WE WERE LIVING in a large house with a basement. Even then, my mother and father worked two jobs apiece just to make ends meet and take care of the family. I remember whenever Mom and Dad came home, we would all sit down in the living room and watch the evening news. It was on such an evening when the newsman announced an abduction, and a picture of the missing girl flashed across the screen. I was a very young child, about five at the time, but not too stupid to notice how quiet the room got. My mother asked us if anyone knew who she was, specifically my brothers who by now were shifting in their seats uncomfortably. They pretended they didn't know. Every day, they showed this missing girl on the evening news. Someone wanted to find this girl really bad, and my mother would always pray for her family hoping that they would find their daughter soon. My mother always had a soft spot in her heart for other people's children, as we all knew that if someone wasn't found quickly, they wouldn't be found alive.

About two weeks after this all started, my mother was taking her lunch break when there was a special newsbreak on the television. She was only able to catch a glimpse of what was going on. All she knew was they had just found the missing girl. My mother was so happy for the girl's family that she was shedding tears of joy, and she started praising God right then and there. You see, my mother has always been a very religious woman, and she always told us we should call on God whenever we had a problem. The news was the talk of the town, and that evening, it seemed everyone in Denver was happy that the girl had been found alive.

As my mother and her coworkers carpooled on their drive home, it was all they could talk about and were wondering where the girl was found. No one knew yet because they had only caught a glimpse of it on the break room TV. Set. As they came within a mile or two of our neighborhood and dropping off my mother, they saw police cars speed past them and wondered where the police were going. They were still talking about the missing girl when the next thing they knew the SWAT team sped past them. My mother said to her friends, "Oh, dear god, I hope no one I know is hurt or anything." My mother knew most of the people in the area they were approaching. Within minutes of her statement, five news station vans jetted past them at high speeds. My mother told her friends, "Oh, dear God, something very bad must have happened!" They had never seen this much action going on at one time. Now they were three blocks away from our house, and all the streets were blocked off. My mother and her friends could not get through, and they did not have a clue as to what was going on. So my mother and her friends walked over to the pay phones to call my father and let him know that something very bad was happening. She told him she had not been to the house yet because it was blocked off. They were going to have to walk to the house, and she would call him back at work to let him know everything was okay once she got home and checked things out. She was not getting an answer when she called the house, only a busy signal. She knew one of the kids was just on the phone talking to some guy or a silly girl. My brothers and sisters lived on the phones, and she was always on to them about staying on the phones.

My mother and one of her friends started their journey toward the house. They just happened to ask a bystander what was going on. The bystander told them that the guys who kidnapped that girl had been found and were having a standoff with the SWAT team. As a result, no one was allowed to go down that way.

My mother began to get scared and went up to a police officer. She told him her children were down there. He answered, "Lady, they have evacuated the area so you do not have anything to worry about." My mother had a strange feeling. All she knew was that she had to get home right away, so she began to run through the crowd with her friend right behind her. When she got closer to the house, she told her friend, "Oh, Lord, they are all at my house!"

The SWAT team had our house surrounded, and the police were talking on a loud speaker, trying to make deals with my brothers to give themselves and the girl up. By this time, my mother started screaming out in a loud voice, "Please, please do not kill my babies!" over and over again. Somehow she convinced the police chief that she could handle it and that there was no need for any violence. She asked them to allow her to go inside and talk to them. The chief allowed it. My mother went in the house, and believe me, she did not spare the rod. She most definitely did not believe in spoiling the child. By the time she was done, my brothers called out to the police for help! All I can say is that Mike Tyson would have met his match in my mama that day.

My brothers knew they would be safer behind bars, especially since my dad was getting off in two more hours, and they would really get it as soon as he got home. My dad had twenty-five-inch biceps; we called them guns because he was built like the iron man from working most of his life in construction. He even looked like he ate gravel for breakfast. He was one dude that you did not want to deal with the wrong way.

When the police saw my mother coming off the third rope on my brothers, dropping her Triple H's on them, the SWAT team and the police thought this was the funniest thing that they had ever seen. The way she was puttin' that ass whippin' on my brothers, I think my mother must have missed her calling and should have been a professional wrestler. My three brothers were begging the police to stop her, and it was the first time I really think they absolutely did not want to get out of going to jail. Plus they knew they had another ass whippin' coming from my father and wanted to plead with the DA for at least twenty-five years. Maybe Dad would cool off by that time.

As far as this missing girl went, what happened was these fools had kidnapped her and had her hiding out in our basement closet. Capone, Boo-da-man, and Heroin had her holed up there for nearly a month. Capone and Boo-da-man were actually the ones who kidnapped the girl. But once Heroin found out what was going on, he was down with them. He even called himself going with the girl after about two weeks. This girl was so delusional that after the kidnapping was over, she still insisted that she was in love with my brother Heroin. These fools would steal packs of bologna and hot dogs to feed this girl for a whole month. How in the world can you fall in love with an idiot who kidnapped and kept you in a closet and fed you that crap for a month? The girl wound up going to the DA and telling him that she wanted her man released because he didn't do anything wrong. She told the DA that she wanted her man back, and that she ran away from home. My brothers just let her stay there. She refused to press charges because she didn't want her man in jail.

The DA agent knew he didn't have a case without her pressing charges or testifying as a witness. If her story hit the surface, he would be the laughing stock of the police force and couldn't jeopardize the reputation he was trying to make for himself.

When he paid my brothers a visit in their holding cell, they were not trying to hear that they were being set free because they knew my dad hadn't cooled off yet. They begged the DA to let them stay there for at least a couple more days. They could not believe this girl went to him and lied about what happened. In spite of it all, the DA threw them out of jail because he was angry and at least wanted some form of punishment for my brothers. I think he really knew the girl was lying, but without her, he had nothing.

My brothers figured that the only way they could straighten it out with my parents was to have the girl tell them the story she had made up for the DA and apologize to my parents for putting them out on a limb like that. Without hesitation, she did just that! She was so sprung on my brother. It was almost pathetic. Where was the justice? But one thing I can say, my brothers had juice with the hood and the ladies. They didn't even need to do most of the stuff they did, they just did it.

The DA agent didn't like what happened with that situation and conspired with the governor who claimed to have proof that there were at least seventy-six felonies between the three of my brothers, but they did not have enough evidence to arrest them and charge them; however, they knew for a fact that they were definitely involved in a lot of things that were going on in the city. So they came up with the so-called plea bargain for my whole family, signed by the mayor of Denver. It was said that if my mother and father agreed to move out of the state with all of their children, they would forget all the alleged conspiracies that they were contemplating against my family. My parents didn't want anything bad to happen to their children, so they agreed that they would leave. That would mean that my mother and father had to pack up a family of fifteen, quit all of their jobs, and get out of town within two weeks. This wasn't an easy task. It took two very seriously strong individuals to accomplish this and still keep a positive outlook on the futures of their family and life without giving up on themselves. The one thing my parents did was that they wouldn't give up on anyone of us. It was all for one and one for all, like the three musketeers except we were seventeen in all, my parents included.

My brothers found out about the forced exodus and called a meeting in the park. It was a gang thing too. My brothers and cousins ran it, and whenever they called a meeting, there were at least two hundred soldiers from the hood who attended. When my brothers spoke, the hood listened. Everyone of their thugsters were upset that my family had to leave the state. So they blocked off the streets and had a going-away block party. No one could get up or down the streets for three days. This put the police force on edge, but the hood didn't care.

Two weeks later, when we packed up my parent's station wagon and the moving truck, the police department assisted us like we were dignitaries. At least that's how it appeared in the eyes of a five-year-old. We had two police cars in front of us and two behind us, escorting us to the state line. Me and all of my brothers thought we were big ballers, but it was a huge embarrassment to my parents. They did not like it at all. But as a young kid, I loved to watch the beautiful lights twirl. So once we got to the Colorado state line, we received a salute and were handed a letter from the governor and mayor's offices asking us to please never return.

3

CITY BOYS

MY FATHER HAD a family in Kansas City, and we were going to move there. So on our way to Kansas, my mother wanted to stop through the state of Oklahoma and visit some family she had there. It was on the way anyway, and we had to pick up my brother Lefty, who was spending a little time with one of my great aunts. We made it to Oklahoma, and it was a very strange place. There was no type of big city life like Denver. It was all country. Me and my brothers were like, "What is all this?"

They had stuff like horses, cows, chickens, and pigs around. We thought it was some really cool stuff because we had never seen anything like that. Where we were from, it was big city life, and there weren't any type of animals besides some of the ugly street rats in the hood.

So this place was dope to us. The only thing though was that the pigs and some of the animals stunk like crap. But as a young boy, this type of thing was exciting. Til I met this damn thing called a horse. I did not know anything about this thing. How was I supposed to know you weren't supposed to walk behind this animal? This was the first time I had ever set eyes on one of these animals. Besides, all I wanted to do, like every other kid in America, was to be like the Lone Ranger. So I walked behind the horse and was going to try to do what the Lone Ranger did. You know, jump on top of the horse without touching the saddle. So my brother called me as soon as I walked behind this horse. He was making me mad; you never step in the way of a kid on his way to becoming the Lone Ranger. That is one thing you just did not do. So as soon as I turned around to see what he wanted, all of a sudden, I was flying the other direction, just that quick.

My face was stuck in the dirt just like an ostrich. We were in the middle of the rodeo grounds that my aunt and uncle owned. I did not know what had happened. All I knew was that my head was hurting like crazy, and there was blood everywhere. My brothers did not want to carry me back to the house like that. They knew we would be in trouble since we were told not to walk down into the rodeo grounds arena and get in there with the mean bulls and wild horses. But you know, telling a boy not to do something is just like telling him to do it. They had no choice but to carry me to the house because I was really losing a lot of blood.

Just like my brothers knew, they got beat down. They took me straight to the hospital and I got about one hundred stitches. I think this was discipline enough for me. I also learned not to walk behind horses the hard way. So now after that drama, we finally made it back to my aunt's house. My mother told me and my brother to stay on the porch so we would stay out of trouble. So we were chilling on the porch and my mother told us point-blank not to get on the rails because they were weak and we would fall off. Now why did she tell us about that? You know, we were just waiting for her to stop paying attention so that we could climb the rails. There was a pile of broken-down bike frames on the side of the porch, and this porch was about ten feet from the ground.

So now my mother's attention was being detained by my aunts and relatives. So me and my brothers were all over the rails. Now we were trying to see who could stand straight up at the top. Now remember the porch was about ten feet in the air, and the railing at the top of it was about an additional five feet, so we were up there. So you know me, I can't let my brother outdo me. I was headed to the top, and that is exactly where I went. I was so cool. I was at the top. I made it, and I stood up tall looking over everything. My brother said I won. He knew my mother was coming, but I didn't. All I knew was that I was the king of the world. And then the next thing I heard was, "Terry, what is going on!" That scared the crap out of me. I knew whose voice that was. The next thing I knew, I was flying. Then all of a sudden, I felt pain in my head. Again, I heard my mother screaming and crying, "My baby, my baby!" I tried to move but one of the bike pedals was stuck deep in my head.

Back to the hospital I went. My mother was hysterical. All she knew was her little boy was not having the best of luck. So I went back to the needle and thread; yes, more stitches. At this time, I was feeling like a pin cushion. But we made it through all this again and made it back home. I walked over to my mother with tears in my eyes, all bandaged up, looking like I had been fighting World War III and only five years old. I told my mother that a giant cat kicked me in the head and now this bike pedal had stuck in my head. I felt like I had seen enough of this country place called Oklahoma. I said, "Momma, when are you carrying me back home? Are you going to wait 'til this place kills me?"

How could my mother tell me that we did not have a home anymore? We couldn't go back to the place that was home to me now. How do you explain that and make a five-year-old truly understand? You know how little kids are. All my mother could do was hug me and kind of smile because I called the horse a giant cat. She thought that was so cute. But she was still unhappy that she couldn't carry me back, I could sense that. But I guess at that time, I just needed her love and hugs. So while my drama was going on, I guess you can say my unlucky streak was like a decoy for my other brothers.

4

DEJA VU

BOO-DA-MAN HAD HOOKED up with some other little country boys in that town. You know that old saying, "Don't judge a book by its cover," believe that. This place seemed like it was so vacant and slow. It was like there weren't any type of hustlers besides my brothers living there. Man, let me tell you, small towns are the worst. Criminals can actually mastermind in the Mayberry USA's of the world, there is a lot of open land where someone can be buried without anyone's notice. These are the spots that most criminals dream of. It's like a gold mine as long as you don't get caught. Well, back to my brother's hustlin'.

There were cats that Boo-da-man met while talking all that gangsta jive about how they wanted to get paid. They didn't know that they were talking to the wrong dude. You see with my family, never talk about something unless you are going to back it up, because with my family, you would have to do just that. Boo-da-man convinced them that if they wanted to get paid, they had to go take it. They looked at him like he was crazy, and they were leery of him. They did not know whether he was serious or not and had no clue as to how down my family was when it came to street games. By law, we were the illest. Truthfully, these dudes were just poppin' off at the mouth. They really didn't know what they were talking themselves into. But like most, they were sticking their big feet in their mouths. So my brother had it all planned out and told these fools exactly how they were going to do it since we're well known for masterminding and carrying things out which was exactly the reason why we were homeless and could never return to where I was born. You could really tell these fakers didn't want to handle this business, still they wanted my brother to think that they had game and some heart. Now remember, these are the types that get pulled into things easily. They were wannabe G's that were getting ready to be put to the test. So now they were at the point of no turning back. It was going down whether they wanted to turn it around or not. Now they know too much, and there was no way they could continue to breathe without going through this mission. That's just how it was.

So it goes down. A perfectly planned robbery, masterminded by my brother. You know these fools actually got away for a minute until they went their separate directions. What my brother didn't know? These busta's didn't know how to keep their mouths closed. They went to the strip clubs running their mouths to some females about how they got paid. You know, that's how most either get killed or busted, 99.9 percent of the time. It's always behind a woman. Low and behold, one of these strippers was an informant trying to get the low down on a hot crime tip to beat her own damn case.

This was like a Christmas gift that came early this year. Damn it! This girl had to 'say it' just like Millie Jackson and more.

Man, the police got after these fools. Now the hunt was on my brother and these fools were considered armed and dangerous. Do not try to apprehend them; shoot to kill were the orders for the force. So after they split up, the cops chased one out of the three down the railroad tracks and blew his lungs out through his chest. His scary partner had his mother call the police force for a plea bargain and turned state on my brother. He claimed that my brother was the one that planned it out and forced them to do it. Now the police were turning over everything to find Boo-da-man, and they were not planning on taking him in alive. You got to understand, this was the dirty south, and during the '70s, racism was out of control. All they wanted to do was kill a brother. That's all these redneck bastards lived for. So what they called it was a "coon hunt" and it was on for them.

My mother knew they were going to kill her son, so my aunt found us a good attorney and made arrangements to bring my brother in to save his life from these klansmen dressed like cops. That really pissed them off. They were betting on who would bring the dead "coon" in. When the attorney brought him in, they all lost, and no Negro was killed. To them, that was a sin. In retribution they gave my brother twenty-five years. My brother stood up and told the judge, "You punks I don't care if you give me fifteen years!" The judge gave my brother a puzzled look and said, "Very well then, twenty-five it shall be." He picked up his gavel and slammed it down.

I have never seen my mother cry like that, ever. It was like the world had ended. I was too young to truly understand what was going on at the time, but one thing I did know was that my mother was hurt very, very badly behind this. She even had a heart attack, and had to be rushed to the hospital. I had to stay with my father and my aunt for a few weeks. To me, you don't take a little brother's mother from him like that. I knew it had to be very serious.

5

A NEW HOME

EVENTUALLY, EVERYTHING WENT back to normal. My mother was back on her feet and better, thank god. Remember, we were supposed to be on our way to Kansas City, but since this happened to Boo-da-man, all of our plans had changed. My mother told my father that there was no way in the world that she was going to leave one of her children behind like that. And my father loved my mother so much that he truly understood.

My father knew all that my mother had been through in her lifetime. I guess you can say he was like her knight in shining armor. God had put my father in her life for a very good reason. That reason was to help her and to protect and love her unconditionally. That is just what he did. You could say he was her guardian angel. So he began looking for a house here in this countrified—deserted-looking town and he eventually found a shell of a house. He was a construction worker so he had building skills anyway. He and my mother felt like they could build this place together and make it into the perfect home.

My parents also felt that maybe it would be better to try to raise us in a slower environment because we were so hyper. Maybe they could try and teach us about country living, you know, to try to get our focus on other things. Then maybe, just maybe we would not get in as much trouble. They knew that something about us seeing animals for the first time had really gotten our attention. They thought if they were to purchase some stuff like that, it would pull our attention away from bad things. Well maybe for some of the younger boys but not the older ones.

6

MORE TROUBLE

MY OLDER BROTHER started running a big time heroin, cocaine, weed, and PCP ring that's how he got the nickname Heroin. He was considered what we would label today a baller. One of my other brothers thought he was Al Capone. He absolutely did not care or have any type of respect for life. He was treacherous and had a very clever mind, as the saying goes, "A mind is a terrible thing to waste." He was the poster boy for it; he also loved hitting people in the head with bumper jacks.

But I loved all of my brothers. I can remember Capone was so brilliant. He introduced Oklahoma to credit card hustlin' schemes and masterminded big moneymaking schemes. All he ever watched on television was the news and the stock market. You better believe he made big money. If he got a little low on his cash flow, he and his mob would just go out and hit a lick and I am not talking about petty crimes here. I am talking big time capers.

Whenever Capone was around, you never had to worry about anything. Money was never a problem. He used to buy us all types of suits, cashmere coats, gator shoes, and godfather hats. He would buy my sister's brand-new wardrobes and always stuck about four or five hundred in your pocket. He never really cared about the money. I think he only wanted to see his family happy because he knew how poor we were and what we had been through. He wanted us to see and experience a different part of life. You know, for some of the youngsters like us, we thought that was pretty fly.

But my parents were always totally against it. My father didn't allow it at all. We had to sneak a lot of things into the house. We always kept things that were going on in the household from him because we knew he wasn't going for it. But my mother on the other hand, we all knew how to turn on our mother's affectionate side and manipulate the situation. A mother will stay fooled behind the love of her child. We all knew how to make her look into our eyes, giving her that look. Most of the time, she would fall for it and cover for us. So I guess you can say we had our mother kind of on lock sometimes. It seemed like things were slowing down and going really well. But you know nothing ever lasts forever.

My brothers all started getting busted by the law for the things they were doing. Heroin had been caught with his huge drug ring. Lefty was going in and out of the penitentiary for all of his DUIs. Popeye was in for manslaughter. I can't even remember what Capone got picked up for. But they all ended up going in and out of the penitentiaries like clock work. It was unbelievable. Sometimes I can remember having to walk out of one courtroom, then walk right down the hall to another and around the corner to another. That's how much trouble they were all in.

My mother's new job became being down at the courthouse, going from one courtroom to another. Now this was way too much pain for a beautiful, strong woman like my mother to have to go through. Every courtroom we went to, the judge gave each and every one of her babies some time. Every time the judge dropped his gavel, my mother flinched and cried. I remember Momma holding my hand with her head down and just about dragging her purse in the other hand. She was just about cried out by the end of the day. She would say in a low tone, just loud enough for both of us to hear. "Father, please give me strength. Father, please give me strength." Then she would say, "I love you, Father," over and over in a tired, weary voice. I was just a little kid. I did not see anybody around, and I knew my name was not Father.

I knew my father was at work, and I told my mother, "Momma, Daddy is at work."

She said, "Yea, baby, I know."

"Momma, you are not supposed to talk to yourself."

"Baby, I was talking to the man upstairs."

"Where are the stairs at?"

"He is in the clouds up above."

I looked up and scratched my head for a minute and then I said, "Momma, are you going crazy like the lady on your soap operas?"

My mother looked down at me and just laughed, and then she hugged me. You see, even at your lowest time, it seems in life God has a way of bringing your spirits some joy. Sometimes he will send it through little kids, like myself with a speech problem. That just made my mother happy again for a few minutes, and I got a loving hug because I was tired too. We went home without my brothers. All five of them, Boo-da-man, Heroin, Lefty, Popeye, and Capone. they had new homes for at least the next ten years apiece.

All of this was incredibly hard for both of my parents. They were dealing with the pain and embarrassment of literally being thrown out of our hometown. With that, they had to find a way to survive and provide for fifteen children. It seemed like there was nothing but wave after wave of stress, knocking them down and drowning them. My parents are not only the most honest, kind, and humble people I know, they're also the strongest. They loved God. And he gave them the strength to go on with their lives for the sake of all of their children. They worked hard and found ways to make our lives better, while they tried to keep us from repeating the mistakes of our older brothers.

7
COUNTRY BOYS

A S TIME WENT by, my father brought us some chickens, pigs, and cows, and my uncle Billy Ray started giving each of us horses. We loved our uncle so much. Every kid on the block wanted a horse. But we didn't get just any horse, we were all getting quarter horses which made us feel special. You see, my uncle owned a stable of racehorses, and he loved horses just like we did. So he made sure that we had some horses too. That was so cool. My father began to teach us work ethics, how to take care of animals, grow our own food, and to be responsible. He gave us all daily chores: feeding animals, picking up eggs from the chicken pens, and watering the animals and the gardens. Yeah, my father had turned us big city boys into country boys, and it was fun for a while. Until we started getting lazy and wanted to play sports or hang out with the hood kids. But Daddy told us point-blank, you better do your chores before you go anywhere and that includes sports, friends, etc., before the day ended or our butts were the grass and he was the lawnmower. My father never repeats himself twice and we knew it. Once was all he told us, and that was all we needed. My father was huge like Rudy's father on the *Fat Albert Show*; you didn't want to get hit by one of his enormous hands. My father's hands were so rough that one time he rubbed his hand across my face, and I thought my skin would come off. We used to sit with my father on Saturday, watching championship wrestling, we'd just be sitting there watching the action on the screen when suddenly the skin on his fingers would bust open, like Ball Park franks that were already plumped! It came from the concrete work that he did. We were amazed and laughed not realizing how tough it was on his body and that he worked so hard, still we had a lot of fun with my father on the weekends, it was the only time we had to spend with him because he had to work the rest of the time. Me, the homies, and my dad would walk through the house, breaking wind and blame it on my mother and it was the first time I was introduced to the fart game. We thought this game was the funniest thing in the world. My homies loved coming around on the weekends to chill at my pad because my father was also the ragging king. He could talk about you so bad that you would literally start laughing at yourself and the jokes he made about you, so they came over just so he could rag on them.

Most of them didn't have fathers around and it was their way of sharing the love of my father which was cool. My father knew it and treated them like they were his kids too. When we had to go to the farm and work, he made them go too, he would put them to work and they loved it and we'd crack jokes while we worked. A lot of people just don't know how hard we had to work on the farm, we owned 388-acres. Believe it or not, we had to walk the length of it and put a five-stranded barbed wire fence around it. Believe me, this was no joke. We're talking working from sunup to sundown. We walked up and down canyons that looked kind of like the Grand Canyon but not as deep while packing a sixty-pound roll of barbed wire up and down it; not once, but five times each and the wire was constantly sticking you in your legs, arms and your butt too. My friends used to say, "Mr. C, this is no way to treat your company." We would just laugh it off and when we were finished, we still had our chores to do and our friends had to help. At the end of the day, our pay was one of my mother's good hot meals. That was all we needed, so I guess you can say we were full-fledged country boys now. I really loved hay day. We would get up at about five in the morning and go to the hayfield. My father would buy maybe four hundred bails of hay, and we would walk the fields behind the trucks and load the truck with the hay. One of us would drive, two would stack, and the others would throw the bails onto the truck. We really thought we were cowboys. We would do all this before twelve o'clock because then the sun would be a scorcher, so we made sure we got it all done. After that, we would carry the hay back to the farm and unload the truck.

I felt just like we were cowboys from *The Big Valley* and we started watching only cowboy and Indian movies then we'd go outside and portray the characters and the scene's we saw on the shows. Our favorite cowboy was John Wayne in the movie *The Cowboys*. We saw this show as us and our father as John Wayne.

One day, my father bought us BB guns. I think that getting us those guns was one of his biggest mistakes, because we thought we were the cowboys. So instead of us shooting at each other, we waited 'til mom and dad left. We watched our show to get really juiced up; it was like our fix. Then, after they left, we snuck in the back and pretended my mother's chickens were the bad guys. Me and my brothers were lighting those chickens up! Man, we shot up all my mother's chickens.

We had one mean rooster that we hated anyway because he would always chase us. One time, when my youngest brother Fred was alive, he caught him because he was little. He started pecking him, we were already set on getting him for being so mean to us anyway. So me and my brothers were all going to get him all at the same time. Boy, that big red rooster looked at us and we stared at him. Then he puffed his chest out. What the hell did he do that for? We were ready for set trippin' after that move because this was for Fred. We lit him up with our BB guns. Do you know this rooster was like James Bond? He was hard to kill. He actually did backward flips while we were shooting him up and flapped his wings and puffed his chest out again. He gave out a loud sound, *ark-aroo-aroo*, after we had shot him up. We thought this chicken acted like he was possessed by the devil, the look it gave us was the closing scene with Al Pacino in the movie *Scarface* still standing with a belly full of bullets! He was the "Real Deal". What this chicken didn't know was that my brother Tony had a pump BB gun and showed up with his dark shades on and his assassinator hat. He pumped his gun up, the rooster was still, *ark-arooo-arooing* all of a sudden, that crazy bird jumped straight up in the air and came after us. I dropped my gun and took off running just as my brother Tony caught him in mid air with his pump pellet gun. That was the end of that big bad rooster.

Tony was the man until Momma and Daddy got home. When that Chrysler pulled up, we all got as quiet as a church mice. You could have heard a pin drop. Momma and Daddy came into the house, and they read us like books. The first thing that they said was, "What is going on?" We said, "Nuttin' just chillin'." And they knew right then that something wasn't right. It seemed like my mother had a radar built into her head. Every time we did something, it was as if she watched us do it all the while saying to herself, "I am going to let them get it all out of their systems and then I am going to tear their butts up." She went straight to the chicken pen.

We went straight to the bedroom and padding on more clothes. I don't know what my brother Lefty would think because he always went straight to the bathroom and disappeared for hours every time. He had to have the cleanest colon in the family. But this still did not save him. It never failed. Momma waited right beside the door no matter how long it took him, and she would beat his butt. Us, on the other hand, we would just try to pad up and get it over with. But Momma was always one step ahead of the game. She would make us disrobe. Then she tore our butts up. You know, she was set trippin' on us. She really put it down for the chickens that day because it seemed like that whipping lasted two hours. After she got through then it was Daddy's turn to tan our hides. There was no sun shining when those chickens went away that day. Our butts were blue, and it wasn't all because of sadness. Our butts were literally blue, and we knew that we deserved every bit of it.

But we still thought we were the cowboys because that very next day we snuck out to where all of our cattle and horses were. And it was rodeo time. Whoever stayed on the young bulls until we could count to thirty would be the champion. Do you know our dumb asses would actually jump on bulls without a rope or anything?. We tried to ride them just like in the rodeo. I don't think I have to tell you who the crash test dummy in the family was, now do I ? Yes it was yours truly. We scoped out the biggest, craziest black young bull,which my brothers threw me on top of him. I did pretty good for the first ten seconds, but after that, the bull was throwing me so high up in the air I could have made the Olympic team in pole vaulting. I'd do about three sommersaults while air bound then I'd land back on the bull butt backwards. My brothers and the homies would laugh their asses of. I could have sworn I heard them say, "Hey, Chuck, I think I am going to have to give that one an eight." And I'd be back in the air again flipping forwards. I guess you can say boys will be boys because everyone picked a bull and ate dirt just like I did.

By the end of the day, we were pretty good. I was able to stay on at least twenty seconds and I felt like I was on top of my game. I was in up to my ears and looking for the ride of my life when I went after my parent's high-dollar Limousin bull. He wasn't fully grown, but he was still a good size, and he had a hump in his back. This young bull already had a bad reputation and everyone was scared of him except me and my homie Woody. My mother and father had spent a lot of money for this bull. He was used for breeding purposes with the other cattle. We were told to stay away from him because he was dangerous. We didn't care; we were the cowboys. Woody jumped on that bull, and the bull was throwing him all over the place I was laughing so hard because he was skinny and looked so funny like Chris Tucker from *Friday* the movie. That bull had him rolling forwards, backwards and from side to side, his head bouncing up, down and all around like a cork bobbing out of water! Woody and that bull were all over that pen. So now it was my turn. I just knew I was a professional bull rider. I walked over to the pen like I was the Man. I jumped on that bull, and I was riding that mean old cuss like it was my job! I went passed the thirty-second mark. I was the bull-riding champion, and I was still hanging on. Woody was cheering me on saying, "Ride! Terry, ride!" I was doing it until I noticed, all of a sudden, I did not hear Woody anymore. So I looked back and Woody had taken off running and the only one there was my mother.

She had a switch. I thought it was one switch, but it was three switches that were taller than she was, and they were braided together. I knew right then I was out again, and my bull riding days were over. I guess by this time, I had forgotten that I was still on this bull, but the bull didn't. He threw me way up in the air and I landed on my head like an ostrich again. It seemed like as soon as my head stuck in the ground, that three-braided switch was whippin' around me like a snake. Boy, I jumped up out of that dirt. This was the first time I really found out how much of a Native American I was. I learned a very big part of my Indian heritage. I learned how to do my own version of the rain dance and probably invented a few new dances. Boy, my mother must have been a cow herder in her previous life. She was working those switches like a bullwhip, I think, that day, me and my mother really invented low riding. She knew how to hit them switches! She had me on three-wheels going front, back, and side to side. I think my homeboy Hector must have been sitting on the fence watching and laughing incognito, and must have gone back to his brothers, uncles, and cousins and told them how my mother was hitting switches on my backside. Then they mimicked what she did to me while driving a sixty-four Chevy. To this day I feel like my mamma and I should have made money off her butt whipping that inspired 'Low Rider's! Now that's why me and Hector don't see eye to eye to this day!

As time went on, I decided I was going to be good. I was a new man, rehabilitated up until that very next day. I had to retire my bull riding career due to some technical reasons—my butt was on fire. I decided that we were going to become some championship hog riders. We learned not to mess with my mother and father's animals anymore. For some reason, every time we did, I would get this terrible aching pain in my backside.

With this new plan, we knew a man two blocks away who had some giant hogs. We also knew he went to work at about four in the evening because we had watched him prior to making this decision. We were planning on riding his hogs anyway. You got me. So me and the homies were gonna go test our riding skills on the giant hogs. These giant hogs were crazy. They bucked harder than the bulls did. They would run you straight into the walls of the pens, trying to kill you. They were hollering and screaming in their own language and in the end we were all doing the ostrich look again. And just when we thought we could get away that old man started shooting at us. Evidently he did not go to work that day. He must have had a feeling that we were trying to steal his hogs. We were just some kids trying to have a little fun. That day was the first time we all realized, that we had a really good track game. Somehow, before I even got home, my mother and her radar senses had found out everything. I was like damn, *How is she finding out every move I am making?*

As soon as I got home, I thought I was cool. I walked through that door, man, another switch hit me and twisted me around like a tornado. I'm sure that day we invented the Twister. I know the writers from the movie *Twister* owe me a few ends. I guess they don't want to pay a brother either but that's cool too. So I decided from now on, the only things I was going to ride were my horses and my bike because this was not the life for me.

8

A CHANGED MAN

I DECIDED THAT instead of engaging in activity that caused me physical pain (in my backside), I'd start really getting into sports. I started playing baseball with most of the homies in the hood. They were doing it to get juice with the girls. I was doing it just because I liked the sport. I was playing center field, but my batting average was not up to where it should have been. But all I can say is that I had some really good coaches. They really cared about their players. One of them was named Poncho. He was so cool that he would even come and pick me up for practice since he knew my father was at work all the time. Poncho really cared about all of his players, so that was cool. My other coach was James Hill. They loved me and the rest of the players; we were just like a big family. I owe them a lot, and I will never forget them.

James and Poncho would make me work on my batting because they knew I needed help in this area. They discovered that I had a seeing problem and told my mother and father. Did you know that after my mother and my father carried me and got me some glasses, I became the home run kid. Man, it was really cool. My coaches were so proud of me, and they did not know how proud I was of them just for being there for me. If I could, I would go and let them know right now. I guess that's what I am doing with writing this book. I hope they are around in spirit to know this. I found out that they are both deceased. So I still want them to know that I love them and to say thank you.

So my game got better and better. Then one day, my brother Tony, who was one of the best pitchers in the state of Oklahoma. Everyone wanted to get him on their team. For that reason alone, no one could hit this boy's fastballs or curves. This boy would throw the ball so fast and hard that he could hardly find anyone to play catcher when he pitched. When the ball hit that big old padded bat catcher's glove, you could feel it. Man, that hurt like the Dickens! That boy had one hell of an arm. He showed me that I had a pretty good arm myself. Tony worked with me all day on my pitching and taught me his special curve ball.

By the time Poncho came to pick me up for practice, I was so proud of myself and my brother teaching me his gift. I'd say, "Poncho," with a big smile on my face, "you have to see this." He parked his truck right behind Tony. He was bat catching for my pitch while Tony told me what types of pitches to throw. Man, that ball was straight down the plate every time. It was so fast and hard you could hear Tony's glove sounding off. Poncho was amazed he called James and they encouraged me to continue. My brother had turned me into a very well-known pitcher like himself. I knew that it was nothing but brotherly love. I will never forget that.

So from there, I went off to start playing football. With my glasses, I was like a new man that year. I won trophies in almost everything I did. I got best offensive player of the year and best defensive player in football. I won state in wrestling, all city in the 100-yard dash, and placed second in all state in track. In basketball, I received the most valuable player's award.

I even got to the point where I took a California Achievement Test and scored so high that a Marines official and a doctor came to visit me at school. They also gave me an award for it. They wanted me to start attending a class at Presbyterian Hospital for young overachievers who wanted to become doctors. I was supposed to start going there two days a week on Tuesdays and Thursdays at seven o'clock in the evening. This was a very big achievement that most kids could not aspire to. I guess you can say I turned into a nerd. My life was all about making the best grades in the classroom, being the best in all areas of sports, and doing all of my chores so Dad would not get on me.

I know my parents were really proud of me and they would practically buy me whatever I wanted. They really started to support me in the things that I was doing. I felt like the world was mine. I knew I had it all. I was even getting a weekly allowance, which was really big time for me and my brother Tony. My mother was running the community center at the time, and we would even play on her summer league teams. My moms ran the hood. All the kids loved her. The females were all trying to stay close to my mother to get at us. Back then, me and Tony were some of the hottest, and the sexiest teens in Oklahoma. Girls would go nuts when we would go play at other schools or if we just went to other games. They treated us and our cousins like we were some type of movie stars or something.

Tony and my cousins would eat it up because they were all into being mack daddies. But I didn't care for girls. I was still like a nerd, I guess. Man, all these girls would call our house and try and talk to me and Tony. But Tony would kick it with them all. He was a big time player. I would tell them I could not talk to them because I had to slop the hogs and water all the animals. They would just laugh and laugh because they thought I was just playing and cracking jokes. But it was dead serious to me. That is what I had to do before I could go to practice for whatever sport I was playing at that time. I just told them that my daddy did not want me thinking about girls right now, and it wasn't a lie because my dad didn't. He knew how easily a young man could get a little young girl pregnant. I really did and still do look up to what ever my father tells me. I always idolized my father, and I wanted to be just like him. I thought he was the coolest. But I really didn't want to have anything to do with girls at that time. I loved everything else I was doing, and I did not have time for anything else.

9

THEY'RE BACK, THE REUNION

By THIS TIME, all of my brothers began getting out of prison, and that was cool because it had been about ten years since all of my brothers were back together again. My mother and father were going through some serious issues at this time. You see, my mother's past was trying to hunt her down. She had experienced such a bad life that her ex-husband started trying to get her back. Now her ex-husband had cut my mother up and made her a prostitute in the past. She had children by this fool, and my dad was now in the picture. He was my mother's knight in shining armor. He was not going for any of this man's crap, even though this man was the father of a few of my mother's kids. But that meant nothing to my father. In his eyes, he was their father. He never treated any of us like one was better than the other. Believe me, that was how he was. He was such a good man, and he still is to this day.

Since they knew that all of their sons were getting out of the penitentiaries, they knew they needed a place to stay. They owned a few rent houses, and they gave the boys two houses to live in. Like always, they provided for their children with homes of their very own.

While all of this was happening, my parents were still dealing with my mother's ex-husband. This man had cut my mother up and beaten her badly for numerous years. He was calling my mother and father telling them how he was going to kill them. My father was nothing close to some type of chump. He was like, *This punk really don't know what type of a person he is getting himself involved with.* My father's family, the Carneys, are a family in Wichita, Kansas and Texas, that no one would mess with. We were deep, and this is one family that even today most won't mess with. But my mother had kids with this man, and my father respected that, because he loved my mother unconditionally. He didn't want any of us children to know what was actually going on among our family. My mother and father decided that they were going to try to keep it away from the kids and that is just what they did.

So my brothers were about to come back home, and it was cool because me and Tony had gotten so big since they had last seen us. It did not take long before things were back to the way they used to be. My brother, who thought he was Al Capone, was even out again. He was driving down from California, so it was kind of like a big family reunion. What they should have left out of the mix was the drugs and the alcohol. It seemed like almost my entire family was into some type of drugs or alcohol. None of them could ever handle it, and it always got somebody in trouble. They started off with corn whiskey, and we all knew it would be happening very soon after that. At first, it seemed like they were all having a good time. But Capone wanted some heroin; he really loved that crap. So he and my brothers went on their drug spree. My older brother, who had been a big heroin dealer before, was out too. He did his time, but he still had his connections, so this was a family thing. He hooked it up for my brother, and they kicked it and rolled on.

By the time they got back, they began to reminisce. Capone was stuck on some craziness from when they were kids. Capone was jealous because he thought that the women always loved my older brother Heroin. He claimed that he felt Heroin always thought he was better than everyone else. He was still pissed because Heroin used to be really good at martial arts. He always kicked Capone and the rest of my brother's asses. Capone felt like he was bigger now, and he wanted his revenge. These fools went out and bought more corn whiskey, and we knew the heat was on. It wouldn't be long.

Capone got that look in his eye, and he started calling my other brother all kinds of punk's and it was on. Man, they went back to their teenage days. They started breaking down in their kung fu stances. It was totally off the hook. They were acting like they were younger than me. I had to laugh at first. Then it broke into a saloon brawl. They were breaking chairs over each other's heads. Heroin was boiling some water on the stove and tried to throw it at Capone. It ended up hitting my brother Popeye. Then he socked Heroin. Capone got mad and asked Popeye what was wrong with him, and he socked him for hitting Heroin. Man, everybody was just hitting each other. This was some fun entertainment for a youngster, they were flying through windows and glass screen doors, just like on TV. When they would fly out of the window through the glass or the door, they would jump straight up and run right back in there and continue to fight.

This was the funniest thing we had ever gotten together and done as brothers. That was until Capone picked up the brand-new boom box that I got from Mom and Dad for Christmas. It had an eight-track player on it and a double cassette. It was the bomb. He picked it up and hit my brother over the head with it. It just broke into pieces, and I socked him. Now that really pissed me off because I really loved that box. But not anymore, it was demolished. Tables were flying and breaking over our heads. It was on and the house was destroyed. And believe it or not, this was a great family reunion to me because I loved my brothers. To me, this was nothing but great family love.

Now this is what really got me. Some man stopped by and yelled, "You all stop before someone gets seriously hurt."

I really don't think this man knew who he was dealing with. You never get yourself involved in a family discussion. We never allow outsiders in our discussions. Man, everybody stopped and looked at this fool and just started beating him down; somehow he got out of that door, or we threw him out the window and he took out running. We could not catch that fool. He was like Jesse Owens, the fastest dude I have ever seen. Then after we were done for the day, everybody got scared. We knew Daddy was going to kick all of our butts. So they went out and brought new windows and doors and fixed everything.

10

GOD BLESS OUR HAPPY HOME

For me, it was the beginning of one big happy family. But do you know the same thing began to happen day after day? It was like a rerun for about a month. I finally had to tell my brother Tony, "Man, you know what, I am really tired of fighting." He said, "Man, I am really tired of fighting too." He also told my brother Popeye that he was tired of fighting. He said the same thing. But it did not stop Capone and the rest of our brothers. I would drive down the street daily and my brother Boo-da-man would flag me and my other brothers through and tell us that it was jumping off with his hand language and laughing. We knew what he was saying, and if we didn't feel like fighting any of those days, we would simply keep on driving. But if we were tense and needed to get some stress out, we would stop just to let some tension off, go into the saloon and fight.

That lasted for about two months and then it was time to start getting paid. Even though my parents had raised us to be honest and hardworking people, my brothers had a different idea about what exactly work was. They didn't believe in the traditional nine-to-five, "would you like paper or plastic, can I supersize that for you" type of work. They wanted big money as quickly as possible, with as little manual labor as possible. They'd go buy a liter of Jack Daniels, drink it, and mastermind a plan for a huge robbery. That's just how it was, and these fools would actually get away with it. I remember when they went and hit one of the Happy Foods convenience stores. They probably got about ten thousand dollars from that lick. We literally watched it on a show they had there called *Crime Stoppers*. It was like the TV show *America's Most Wanted*. We would watch them reenact the robberies that my brothers had committed, and we'd be screaming and hollering, promoting it as if it was the Super Bowl. To my brothers, this was like being an actor or musician or some big-time, underworld celebrity. What they did really meant something big to them. The police and the vice still didn't have a clue. That's what was so messed up. They dedicated their lives to masterminding the law, and that's just what my brothers did. They were what you would probably call untouchable because they knew everything to the point that they could have taught the laws and the police force a thing or two.

After that, it was all over for the time being. It was almost time for my freshman year of high school to start.

My mother and father were still dealing with some of the drama my brother's father was putting down. He was still threatening their lives, and my parents didn't want us to know anything about what was going on. They wanted me to stay with my brothers until everything was over, and they absolutely didn't want any of us involved with any of this crap. They didn't want this man to start separating our family with all his devilishness. Especially since he was the father of some of my brothers, and it would be hard for them to know how to deal with that type of situation. So they kept it all to themselves and dealt with it the best way they knew how. They decided that it was best to separate themselves from the family without starting a war among us. They knew that is exactly what would happen because we were the type of children who looked for something to start set trippin' on.

I remember waking up on the first day of school—my freshman year of high school. My brother Capone and my cousin Sterling were arguing. It was seven o'clock in the morning. I was fourteen years old, fixing myself a bowl of cereal, Frosted Flakes Tony the tiger cereal. And they were up all night hustlin' for their heroin and Jack Daniels addictions. These fools started preparing their drugs right on my cereal table so they could shoot it into their veins. I was just eating, watching my Jackson Five cartoons, trying to listen to Michael talk about how he was going back to Indiana while they were acting crazy as hell.

Sterling got to hollering, "Capone, hurry your ass up with the fix!" Capone would say, "Go to Hell!" That is how they would all talk to each other. That is just how it was, even though we were the best of homies and cousins. Capone got the fix ready and stuck it in his vein. Sterling got pissed off and he said, "Goddamn, Capone! You are taking it all!" I was just eating my cereal and was getting pissed because I was being distracted because Michael was now singing about ABC is easy as 123; ABC, that's how easy love can be. But I was also watching their every move. They really started trippin'. My cousin Sterling began to chase my brother around the breakfast table like they were little kids. He was hollering at Capone saying, "Goddamn it, Capone! You are taking all of it!" Capone would just run around the table, trying to take all the heroin from cousin Sterling. Capone would just laugh and continue to try to take all of the heroin. Then Sterling finally caught up with Capone and snatched the syringe out of Capone's arm and stuck it in his arm.

Man, to me, this was so comical.

Little did I know then the traumatic effects this kind of negative behavior would play in my future. It had already began to shape my decisions with drug use on a subconscious level, and I believe to this day, it was the reason why I never thought twice about repeating what I had seen.

11

THE BIG PAYBACK

THIS WAS KIND of a daily, morning episode for me before I headed off to school. It wasn't very comforting or encouraging. It definitely didn't give me a good start to the day so that I could deal with the normal stress of being a teenager and trying to do my best in school. As time went by, I became more and more interested in this type of lifestyle. I still really wanted and missed the lifestyle that I was used to with my parents. I told my parents that I wanted to change schools and live with them again. They thought that it was best that I stayed were I was, at least for the time being. They still weren't telling us what was really going on. To tell the truth, I wasn't telling them what was really going on in our household. They thought my brothers were being responsible adults. Little did they know, I was pretty much raising myself. They were teaching me everything a fourteen-year-old boy should never know.

All of the wrong type of people were starting to hang out at our house, the same way it used to be. There were murderers, robbers, big-time drug lords, and strawberry's having sex with guys right in the middle of our living room floor. Whenever somebody needed their daily fix, my house was the place to be. Anything and everything that you could imagine was going on right there in our house. My brothers turned my parent's respectable homes into big-time drug houses. It was really crazy.

We had pounds and pounds of weed all hidden in the ceilings and walls of our house. We had a room that we called the 'walls of heroin.' That was exactly what the damn walls were filled with—kilos of cocaine and heroin. Then we also had a room that we called the 'walls of water.' Today people call it 'loop-loop,' or PCP. We had gallons and gallons of of it. The really crazy thing about it all was that my brothers were well known for their construction work. That's exactly what they had done to my mother and father's walls. It was like they were practicing their interior design skills by creating their own idea of designer fashioned walls. The entire time, my parents had no clue to what was going on. If my daddy had found out, he would have killed them all, especially since they were his kids. That wasn't how he had raised them, and my parents did not play the drug game at all. They were honest and respectable people, and they expected nothing less from their children.

They kept me and Tony quiet by telling us that once things were right, they would start paying us too. They would give us a little money, fifty dollars here and there. Being surrounded by drug addicts and killers wasn't what I really wanted for my life, even though most people would find life in the fast lane fascinating. My brothers had any and everything that they wanted, whenever they wanted it. I only wanted my parents and the loving environment that they had always provided for me. After a while, I also wanted my cut of the action. It was wrong that I had to sit around and put up with all of their sick crackheads and murderers, not say a word, and not get anything out of it. I wasn't attracted to my brothers' lifestyles. All that I ever cared about was being smart, athletic, and making my parents proud. But there's no way I was going to put up with them and let them get away with giving me nothing for my part in helping their little operation. My life was miserable, and they owed me for that.

We wanted to make some money like they were making. They were balling like crazy. They knew they had to give me and my brother Tony some shut-up money, or we would have sung like canaries. So they continued to give us kibbles and bits. Tony believed that one day they were going to hook us up with some more loot. But I knew better. A few months went by and every time we would ask them when they were going to start kickin' us down, they would give us some more little money. So I was really getting tired of all this, but Tony was still cool with it. You have to understand that I had watched all these fools grow up. I saw how they would play people. Someone had to play

Bounty superabsorbent and pick all the game up, I was it. I paid full attention to anything that you did around me and learned it. I just sat back and thought, *All right, this is cool. These fools think we're dumb.*

Now I was set trippin' on my own brothers. I wouldn't even tell Tony what I was getting ready to plan out. I just kept it to myself. That way, I didn't have to worry about him telling them what I was up to. I also didn't want him telling them what I had done once I had started doing it. So mum's the word. You see, I have always been the type of hustler that never told a soul if I was going to do something. My big brother Capone use to preach to me about that all the time. That's how he was. He did not trust nobody. He knew they would always rat you out, and he would always be left doing dirt all by himself. That's exactly how I feel to this day. I do not trust anyone, whether they're friends or family. I kept my eye on the sparrow, just like *Baretta*.

I started sitting back and thinking of the perfect plan. You have to understand they were brilliant. I really had to come up with a genius plan in order to pull this caper off. I really shouldn't have been planning on robbing my very own brothers. It was really crazy. My brothers were giving me money and everything. I had more money than any of the youngsters in school, my age, and older. I don't think it was really about the money after I've sat down and analyzed the situation.

I was just really angry at my parents for leaving me with these nuts. I didn't like the environment that they had left me in. If I had told them what was going on, they definitely would have come and got me away from there. But that would have gotten my brothers in trouble and thrown out of the houses. I could not snitch on them. It was like a brother's oath of secrecy that we believed in. A G code. So I had to keep quiet and miserable.

I guess this was my way of starting to get rebellious. This was the beginning of me as a young kid, actually crying out for help. I wanted my mother and father, and I didn't know what to do to get them back. The only thing that I could think of was to start messing up in school. I didn't know that I was doing it for that reason exactly then, but all I did know was that I was angry about it.

My brothers would be the first to start paying for my anger. I felt that if it weren't for them, my life wouldn't have changed into misery. In my eyes, it was on now. I stayed up all night, planning and plotting. I finally came up with the perfect caper. My plan was so proper that I had amazed myself, and I was ready to put it into action. Every morning, they got up and had a meeting in their room. One would leave to pick up more supplies and the other would stay to handle the business. They did this like clockwork. I had the joint cased down to the T. They shouldn't have messed with me or assumed that I was stupid just because I was only fourteen. I knew that sooner or later, one of them was leaving to go get the supplies and bingo. Just like I expected Boo-da-man was going to pick up the supplies today. That meant that my brother Popeye was going to be the contestant on my version of the Price is Right. I sat in front of the TV watching cartoons, just waiting for him to go take his morning crap. I knew it was going down very soon because Popeye always went around that time. So when mother nature called, I started my gangsta move. He was off just like the horses. He went and did his thing, so I had to do mine.

I jumped up, snuck right into the powder room to freshen up with the good smell of herbs and spices, and bingo! That room was a junkie's heaven. It had all the trimmings, just like Thanksgiving. I knew I only had a little time so I unlocked one of the windows. I knew they wouldn't check because there was a dresser partly covering it. Plus, they had so many other things going on that they wouldn't even pay attention to it. That was their biggest mistake. I quickly unlocked it and considered it my first checkmate. I ran out of the room and went back to watching cartoons just as if I had never moved from my spot. Right after I did that, Popeye came out. It was like I had escaped by the skin of my teeth. He didn't suspect anything. He thought I was in a trance watching my cartoons as usual. Little did he know that all hell was about to break loose. I knew that Boo-da-man was coming home soon because it only took about thirty minutes to get the supplies and return. It was a daily adventure, and I knew it like the back of my hand. I was laughing my butt off on the inside, but the drama was just beginning.

When Boo-da-man came back home, he and Popeye started handling their business. I knew that as soon as they had a meeting, they would have to go pick up another super big shipment. When that happened, I called up one of the homies who was like my right-hand man. We kicked it like we were brothers. His father was not around so my family practically adopted his big-headed self. We took him under our wings, and if he ever screwed up with anything, my brothers would kick his butt, just like they would have kicked mine. He was in, like that with us. He was also the first friend I met when I moved to Oklahoma. I kicked game down to him, and he came right over. I knew no one would suspect anything because he came over every day to hang with me, so today didn't seem any different.

My brothers locked up the rooms and told me that they were going to work and would be back shortly. That's what they called it because to drug dealers, robbers, murderers, or anyone involved in a criminal profession, that's what it is. It's just as normal as the square folks who go to a nine to five and call it work and those working against the law call what they do a day job just like everyone else. My brothers were off to their jobs, and now I knew how much time I had before they got back. That meant it was time for me to go handle mine. I said to my dog, Big Daddy Buck, "Hey, you ready to go to work?" And he said, "And you know this, man!" So I said, "Let's do this." I made Big Daddy Buck the lookout. I creeped out in my Zorro suit and climbed through the window. I said, "Hmm. Okay, let me see what kind of goodies I want to start with." I took about four pounds of weed and two kilos of cocaine. "Let me see what else I need to add to my shopping list? Oh yea, I need some water to wash all this down with." So I took two gallons of that, and believe me, this is not the type of water somebody would want to drink. But, if you were to dip a cigarette in it and smoke it, it would make you get butt naked and run down the street. I have seen that type of stuff too many times. This was the uncut Bombay! The stuff that straight up did not play. To a square it was PCP.

So I dashed out of the window like good old Saint Nick. I kindly put everything back in place exactly the way it was, closed the window, and put the screen back on. Then me and my homie went off like pirates to bury our treasure. We thought it was so cool. My brothers didn't have a clue. Man, weeks and weeks would go by and every other day, just like clockwork, I was getting over on them. I came through the window like Brotha Man and carried it right back to the 'fifth flo'. They did not know what was hittin' 'em. Boo-da-man thought that Popeye was the culprit, and Capone thought that Boo-da-man was. Between the two of them they never suspected anything. I had turned hardcore, and I couldn't care less. Now I was the man. I was just like an ant, stashing my stuff and saving up for the winter. It was off the hook. I was getting deeper and deeper in the game. To tell you the truth, all this stuff was really fly. I didn't need anything now. But if I could have traded it to get my parents back, I would have given it all up and gone back to being a nerd again. But that didn't happen, and I was still angry.

Everything continued to go on and on. My brothers were so mad at each other that they didn't trust each other at all. They were really ready to kill each other. They even pretty much quit talking to each other, and they were hardly making any profit. They were at each other's throats constantly. They didn't know what was hitting their stash. I had the game on lock. My brothers decided that they had to go their own separate ways because this family business wasn't working out. They split up everything that they had left and started doing their separate hustlin'. That was the end of their business together, and they stayed mad at each other for at least two months. They wouldn't even talk to each other and just knew one had beat the other or vice versa. They totally quit working with each other. They knew they couldn't kill each other over it and that's what was so messed up. They would have never let an outsider do anything like that to either one of them. They wouldn't have lived to tell about it.

They still loved each other and probably still would have killed for each other, but as far as business went, they were not dealing with each other. They were so hot. It was funny to me, but I didn't say a word. I just stacked my treasure. They should have listened to our brother Capone.

He always preached not to trust a soul, twenty-four hours a day. Evidently, no one ever listened to anyone in the house.

I was the last suspect to everyone, I was the baby of the family and I played sponge to everything they would say so how could they defeat me? I was all of them rolled into one. Just like most of the hood movies and ghetto books, the leading character never gets a break. Like always, he goes back to the lifestyle of the poor and unknown. But not for me. I may not have been Santa Claus, but I delivered Christmas to myself with the size of my stash, I didn't really have to worry about too much for a pretty good while. For a fourteen-year-old kid, that was just beginning high school I was making more money than the teachers. I could have employed all of them and believe it or not, I was getting about ten of their checks a year. They were so sprung on that pimp called Snow it had 'em sick. I think that's the pimp of the universe because I was only fourteen, and I hardly had to do any schoolwork. Some of these teachers were so crazy behind Snow, they would give me nothing but As. Some of those maggots thought they could trade sex instead of money. I was like pah-leese! I didn't want their maggot behinds. Just pay me or don't pay me no attention. A lot of people thought I was hard. I just wasn't trying to be played by anybody. I didn't let my brothers play me, so why would I let some teachers play me? I was collecting most of their checks on payday. This was when I really lost respect for school and punk ass teachers.

12

MOONPIE

MY BROTHER TONY thought I was crazy because he knew I had changed so much. He began calling me Moon Pie because people were telling him stories about the stuff I was doing. Me and my brother were close, and in my eyes, we still are. We had spent all of our lives together, and we were all we had. At this time, he started to go off into becoming a pastor, and I was going on. I guess I was turning more and more into Moon Pie. I was getting high, and I wasn't taking no shorts off people that owed me money.

I began to have a crew of about three hundred. You know how it goes when you think that you are the man and wanna-bes come up with that crap like they're your boys or something. People are a trip. They're so fake and full of it. Evidently, they must have thought I had stupid written all over my face, running their stupid games and sad stories when it was time for them to pay up. They would come up with all kinds of stories. I heard some people even started coming up missing, and a lot of weird stuff would start happening to them. I really don't know what was going on because I didn't deal with wanna be's. If you came up to me trying to get at me, I didn't know what you were talking about. People had to go to the homies—La'Money, Hammerhead, or somebody else with that type of madness.

If you wasn't up on game, I wasn't messing with you. My family was the Latin Kings who dwelled all over Chi Town, New York, Miami and Southern Cali. We always told each other to wear that crown high, because kings don't die, we multiplied. While I was going through all that drama, I remember having some fun at the same time. I remember I was in the ninth grade and I had to put my car in the shop; it was messed up. I had to ride the bus, and my brothers wouldn't let me drive their car that day. Me and Big Daddy Buck were at his grandmother's trailer, and she always left early in the morning. We had bought one of those old man pipes, the type that you smoke tobacco in. It had a really deep bowl in it. Man, if a person really wanted to get high, you get one of them and you pack it with nothing but buds. It was about seven thirty in the morning, me and Big Daddy Buck packed it with about three buds and lit it up. It took us on the ride of our lives. I woke up first and then I woke him up and said, "We better get our butts outta here and catch this bus!" We ran out to catch the bus, and man, we sat there for about two minutes to catch the bus to school. I'll be damned, if the bus driver wasn't bringing the kids back home from school! It was totally messed up. I had missed a whole day of school screwing around. But Big Daddy Buck was my dog and it was cool. That pipe was the king of everything the way it laid us down to rest. We were definitely out for a whole ten hours and with all that like, we couldn't wait to hit it again.

So the smoke session started that day! You better believe it. We started having group meetings with anyone that wanted to do business with us, just like my ancestors used to do. I had Big Daddy Buck set up all the meetings at his grandmother's trailer whenever she went to church or something. We loved her so much and she loved us. It was nothing but a family thing, but of course, she didn't know what me and Big Daddy Buck were doing. In her eyes, we were good boys no matter what the neighborhood was saying. We followed my family's tradition and had peace sessions with people that wanted to break bread with us. They had to come there and smoke the peace pipe with us, and no man was able to stand by the time the meetings were over, but us. By this time, Big Daddy Buck was beginning to get used to me. He was starting to be able to handle a lot of the peace pipe that we'd smoke with the clients who were getting ready to climb aboard and join the firm.

Most of the time, we had to pack them out of the office and throw them out on the streets until they would wake up from their journey. These meetings were beginning to become an everyday thing. Everybody wanted to get down with us, but believe me, it was hard as hell to get an appointment. For some reason, the hood stayed loaded off my supply. I can remember when I made it into the book of world records of untold stories. There were all kinds of unreleased hood drama in that book. Mostly because we had done things that hadn't been heard about yet knew I was in it for the bulk of it. These are just a few tales from the 'high hood' episodes.

I remember waking my brother Tony and his brother-in-law Steve up just about every morning. Now Steve thought he could get high and Tony always warned him about me. I was called Moon Pie because I was a sight to see back in those days. I didn't give a damn. I wore my hair in two long thick dookie braids. This was my real hair, not hair weaved like the females had. I also wore cowboy boots with what we called jams that were cut off surfer pants back in the day. Now everybody calls them Bermuda Shorts. I also wore a beat-up cowboy hat and a four-foot-long machete. For all of ya'll that don't know what a machete is, it looks like a sword, but wider from top to bottom. I kept it strapped across my chest like it was a sword. I was well known for chasing people with it, trying to chop their heads off. That is why my brother Tony called me MoonPie because of the way I dressed and the way I acted. They were scared of me back in those days because I was kind of like what little kids would see in a bad dream like Jason or Freddy Krueger.

I would sit back with my brother Tony, reminiscing about the way I looked and acted, and we just laughed and laughed. God must have really had his hand on me back then, and some super prayer worriers had to be praying for me. People really don't have a clue as to what drugs do to kids. I had turned into a product of it all. The truth is, I didn't care about anything—not how I looked, not what people thought about me, not about my life. All I could see was what was around me at the time. I saw drugs and people who didn't care just like me. I really didn't have anything to look forward to or aspire to anymore. When I thought about it and laughed it was not only tragic but my brother was so right. He had picked the perfect name for me because I was crazy and a warped display for people to see. I'm definitely amazed that I survived it all, much less without hurting anyone or becoming a vegetable laid up in some hospital for the rest of my life.

13

THE SMOKE OUT

BACK THEN, THE smoke out was all any of us cared about. My brother-in-law Steve always thought he was the king of getting high. But little did he know, I was his biggest nightmare. I was the one his mother tried to warn him about, but he didn't listen. What makes it so bad is he was about five years older than me and thought that just because he had me in age, he could teach me something. He didn't know that he was in for the lesson of his life. Tony kept trying to tell him, "Man, you better not be trying to keep up with me and MoonPie." He just wouldn't listen. So me, Big Daddy Buck, LaMoney, Hammerhead, and Tony sat in Steve's room.

I rolled up a joint that was the size of a hot link. He gave me a stupid look and said , "Damn, man, what is that?"

Big Daddy Buck and LaMoney said, "You haven't seen nothin' yet. It gets crazy." They knew because it was an everyday thing to them, but Steve was a newcomer. We had to introduce him to the real dog pound. So I handed him that big blunt and told him to fire it up. He fired it up and started coughing up a lung! He damn near died. We were laughing our butts off because he was on his hands and knees just coughing his lungs up. I said, "Ayyy, what's wrong with you? Can't hang with the big boys? Are we too far gone past little Stevie's league?" We just laughed and laughed. We continued to smoke, until we got to the end of that giant hot link joint, how we were ever going to finish smoking it was a conundrum that Unsolved Mysteries would have gladly investigated.

I created a joint out of Tops papers that was three feet long. This tree limb would hit harder than Iron Mike Tyson and it took both hands to hold it. My creation was the king of all kings. To top it off, we needed to air out the room. The apartment looked as if it was on fire. It was so smoky that you couldn't see one foot in front of you.

I walked over, opened a window and smoke started racing out of it. The neighbors actually called the Fire department on us. When they got there, Steve met them outside of the door. He said, "What you want?" They said they had got a call about a fire and by the way, it smells it was the type of fire that they loved to put out. I said, "How much you need?" I gave them about a quarter pound of weed. They were happy, said thank you, and left. You see, the reason I gave it to them was because they are supposed to call the police and report whatever was going on. I was always one step ahead of the game. I knew it, and they knew what I was doing by hooking them up. I was bribing them not to say anything and forget about the call, so in other words they never came again. Believe it or not, everybody can be bought or pursuaded to scratch your back. By this time, the room cleared up about a forth of the way. Everyone was in their own little world.

I said to Steve, "So you want to try to play with the big boys, right, Steve?"

He said, "Big boys? How you spell it?"

I said, "Oh, you got jokes! So fire it up and remember you got to crawl before you can walk."

I handed him that super huge joint. Everyone in the room sat up, and they were trippin'. This was the best we had ever had, and he had to hold it in his hand and just look at it. Then everyone in the room had to get up and hold it in their hands. It was incredible. I had outdone myself. This was some of my best work ever. This is how I had hit the book of world records for the unbelievable. We had to just pass it around, hold it, and look at it. It looked like a giant stick, and I could tell Steve was a little scared of that thing because everyone in there had a crazy look on their face. I said, "What's wrong with you? Are you all going to just sit there amazed and babysit this joint or are you going to fire it up?" The room was quiet because they were already past their limits.

Seeing as I was Moon Pie, and considered the hood's crash test dummy I picked that big stick up and put the heat to it. Man, that joint should've won the heavyweight title of the world. It was hitting me so hard I started coughing up a lung and everybody was thinking to themselves like dayamm! Moon Pie was the Jamaican of the hood because getting high was all I did unless I was asleep. I was a get high cowboy, and I couldn't let that marijuana bronco bust me. I bust broncos. I got to hitting it again and again. That joint was like the rocket that NASA should have the technology to create because it sent me straight to the moon in three seconds flat. I passed it around and everybody began hitting it. All I can tell you is that we felt like we all came back to earth about three weeks later. The next day, I came back over to Steve and Tony's house, and as i knocked incessantly on the front door they started pretending that they weren't at home.

I guess they weren't messing with me anymore. Steve had learned not to hang with Moon Pie like my brother Tony had told him. Do you know they wouldn't smoke with me no more until about three months later? They would only smoke a hot link sized joint with me. They would tell me point-blank that was all they were going to smoke. I wasn't going to kill them so I guess they had really learned a very big lesson. That lesson was, don't do drugs, boys and girls, because drugs and Moon Pie will kill you. That became a public service announcement. I had to go off and find some new friends because my brother Tony and Steve did not want to play with me anymore. I had to carry my reggae somewhere else, but that was cool. I could respect that. If the heat gets too hot for you, you got to get out of the kitchen. That's just what they did. I heard they both had joined church right after that.

14

CAUGHT UP

BUT YOU KNOW, I still continued making my money. I really had it sewed up all over the hood and the school yard. Man, I remember one messed-up day. By this time, I guess the campus police really had it in for me. My name must have been hot on their list, but they had to come up with a plan to try to catch me dead in the act or holding. Then they could at least get me with some type of possession charges. For some reason, every time they busted someone else, my name somehow came up. Just like always, you had your so-called hustlin' snitches that always ran their mouths to get out of the blame for what they had done. I was always told not to play the game if you can't handle everything it has to offer. I stayed true to that and was ready to deal with whatever the consequences were without a doubt. I guess the plan that they had set up was to get my butt early in the morning. As soon as I got to school, I knew someone had to be giving them all of my information. The snitches let them know about the times when I had a large amount of something on me. But little did they know, I always kept a whole lot of something on me. I kept a pound of weed on me each and every day. That was my personal, get-high stash. I didn't care if one of my workers ran out of product and they needed more. They weren't getting any of my smoking stash. That was for me, and nobody was coming between me and my "to get high on sack," which is what I called it.

That morning, I felt some vibes off a few teachers as I walked down the hall on my way to class. Then all I heard was "Terry, stop! You are under arrest." I said, "What," and they had to walk me to the office in order to cuff me. That was the procedure because they had to frisk me before they could cuff me. The rules were that they had to do all that in the office, not in the hallways in front of all my classmates. This was my big break because as you already know I had my "to get high on stash" with me under my coat, and yes, it was a whole pound of weed. I was like what am I going to do now. I can't let them get me like this.

But luckily for me, all the hoodlums that I ran with were in and out of the office just like clockwork. As the police were walking me into the office, I spotted one of my boys on his way out. It was just like he read my mind. We both knew what was up. We had to get the pound of weed out of my coat and to him before they searched me. We hit this move like something you would see on television. It was so dope. We walked right into each other really hard. At the same time, I quickly pulled open my coat and slipped the pound of weed into the inside of his coat. He just continued to walk on out the door. It was so smooth and fast. No one had caught anything. I should have gotten an Oscar for that performance.

My homeboy knew to carry it straight to LaMoney and let him know what was going on, and that is exactly what he did. Of course, you know, he took a little out for his troubles and I didn't mind. He had just saved me from getting about twenty years in the state pen, and that was all the pay he needed. I was cool with that because I had plenty more, and he knew that we were all down for the count. That was all that really mattered. So I escaped the police again, by the skin of my teeth. They carried me into one of the rooms in the office, and I had a really big smile on my face, and one of them said, "Look, he's really got nerves. He's getting ready to go to jail and he's smiling about it." What they didn't know was that I didn't have anything like they thought I did. I wasn't going anywhere. I had a lot to smile about. The joke was on them now. They began to search me, and they didn't find anything. I really had them right where I wanted them. I was thinking lawsuit, and I'm quite sure that they knew this.

They were really beginning to get very angry because nothing was turning up. They got to hollering and screaming at each other, and I started smiling really big. It seemed like that pissed them off even more. They started hollering at me.

"Boy, we are going to get you! Just watch!"

They grabbed me by my hair and slammed me down to the ground. I told them, "You bastards need to miss me with all this abusive crap."

"So you don't like to be abused, right?" One of the cops took his hard steel toe shoes and stuck one boot between my legs, and the other cop put one of his boots in the crease of the back of my neck, and both of them were stepping down hard on it!

I was like, "You punks don't have to be doing all this man! This stuff is uncalled for! Man! Why don't you all leave me alone!"

They kept saying to me, "You think you are one of those smart-ass little Niggers, and we just don't like little smart-ass Niggers that try to make a fool out of us. Believe us, little Nigger, this is far from over." Then one pulled a joint out of his pocket and said to the other one, "Look at what I just found on this Nigger."

I was like, "Man, I just saw you pull that out of your pocket."

"Shut up!" And he stepped on my private parts again.

I screamed and hollered and said, "Cut that out! This ain't cool. If you all are going to carry me to jail, just carry me to jail. You don't have to keep on with all this."

They ended up booking me for the marijuana joint. So they read me my rights and then they cuffed me and put me in the squad car. Then they carried me to jail. I know that I had been messing up, but it was beyond messed up that these racist cops were screwing with me. All I know was, this, cold blooded and needless to say, I needed a joint and they were cutting in on my get-high time. You see, I knew I was only going through processing, and I would probably be out before they even finished. But they were just pissed, and they wanted to teach my black behind a lesson. To me, they weren't teaching me nothin'. But all I was thinking about was, how badly I needed to get high. As soon as I got to the jail, I was calling my brother Boo-da-man. I knew he and Popeye would be there to get me out because my parents couldn't find out about it, or their butts were on the line. They were my guardians, and my parents did not play that.

They rushed down and handled everything and got my butt out so I still had to come back for court. When it was time to go to court three weeks later, Boo-da-man and Popeye went with me. We kept it from my parents, I still don't think they know about this today. But it was cool, my brothers were still there for me. I kind of felt bad because my brothers still didn't have any idea about what I had done to their drugs, I didn't tell them anyway. I kept that to myself, but this was one way they became brothers again. They were back together for this situation and that was all that had mattered. God works in mysterious ways.

So by the time the judge called me to plea my case, I just thought "I am guilty" even though that joint was not mine. I didn't care what they did to me because, in my heart, the worst thing in the world had already happened to me. In my world, nothing else really mattered. I felt nothing could hurt me anymore than not having my mother and father. I was already on my way to destroying my life by not caring about my schooling. Now I was doing drugs, something fierce. The judge suspected that I really didn't care, but he knew the charges were wrong, so he did put me on probation for one year. If I didn't get in any more trouble by then, he would drop it from my records. I was like whatever, grabbed my papers after he signed them, and that was that.

15

STREET HUSTLIN'

I CONTINUED TO run with the homies because, to me, they became like my family. We had to keep things on the down low for a while because the cops were still hot on my trail. Now they had me on paper for a year, so I had to watch myself. I sat back and had to invent a new way to make some quick cash; just like always, I came up with the perfect plan. I was the inventor of the bricks in the box game. What I would do is get the bottom cardboard piece that came with a group of four six-pack of soda. I would take two of those and get some clear cellophane wrapping paper. I got the hardwood floor sticking paper and four long, red bricks—the ones with small holes in them. I took a lot of newspaper and wrapped each of the four red bricks up until they were padded in newspaper. Then I took one of the box tops and put newspaper in the bottom of it. Then I put the padded newspaper bricks in the box side by side. Then I put more newspaper over the top of that, so it got pretty snug. Then I put the box top on and taped the two together. I took the floor wood wrapping paper and wrapped the box up so smooth. It looked almost like a Christmas present without the bows. I cut out pictures of new VCRs and video cameras with the tripods on them. I cut out pictures of each and made the same boxes, but I used one photo per box. Then I taped it on top of each box and wrapped them with clear cellophane wrap. It looked and felt just like it was the real deal. Now I had invented my personal brand of new VCRs for sale. If you wanted to buy a brand-new camcorder with tripods, I had them.

I called up the homies and told them what I did. They couldn't believe it. They even had the nerves to argue me down that my invention was the real thing. Believe it or not, I could have sold them a box of the bricks if I wanted to. That's just how real it looked and felt. I let them open a box so they could see how I did it. They started calling me 'brainiac.' I even came up with the talk to sell the boxes of bricks. I set all of my comrades down and ran it down to them. All you have to do is ride around on days that you know people get paid, like Thursdays, Fridays, Saturdays, and the first, third, and the fifteenth of the month. I told them these days it would be easy to sell. The best places to catch these fools are at the gas stations while they are filling up with gas. You know, they just got paid and cashed their checks. Just act like you are from out of town and you need a little help. Start them out on five hundred dollars for the cameras and two hundred for the VCRs. Tell him you needed to do this because you are trying to get back home. Most of the time, they will try to talk you down, but who cares. Let them roll with what they will pay, and let them have it. Believe it or not the first time and for a while after, I started making about five thousand dollars a week with this game.

I knew to only do it for a while and then leave it alone just like any other game. But not all of my other homies. They were always greedy, and they burned the game all the way out. So, you know, a lot of them started getting caught up and going to jail behind this game. People were really pissed off because they were taking the hard-earned money that they worked for. They thought they were getting a deal and purchasing something that they just knew was a hell of a deal. Then, by the time they got home, they found out that they had just bought a box of bricks. Now I feel bad about a lot of things I invented and did to people, but to me, this was one of the worst. Most of these people weren't the type of people that knew con's like us existed. A lot of them called themselves helping out their fellow brethren, and they were getting something in return. But come to find out, they had just been beat. The lesson for today, little boys and girls, is never gamble on something you can't really see, and buy whatever it is that you want from the store. There are a lot of con artist out in the world, just like I was. But you have to understand that I was just a kid who was deep into the street life and was down by law. That's just how it was.

16

WET DADDY DAYS

WE WERE MAKING enough money that we even started moving up on our drug use, including PCP. We weren't in our right minds half the time anyway, but with this stuff we were baked. PCP was the baddest drug that ever came out. We called it wet daddies. Today they call it loop-loop. So when someone gets looped, he isn't in his right frame of mind at all. I remember one time we were down at this club where we hung out late nights. Everybody was getting wetted out and getting so ill. I remember I took the glass out of the sunroof that I had customized over my backseat. I was chilling. I had smoked about ten daddies. All of a sudden, I looped out. I grabbed my gun and just started shooting out of the sunroof at the stars. Everybody else at the club started cheering me on. That is just how crazy and looped out everybody was. It was about one thirty in the morning too. We all considered this having a good time.

Then all of a sudden, one of the old school homies got looped out to the max and started dancing around. He took off his shirt so we started cheering him on. Everybody started shooting their guns in the air and he was eating it up and was really dancing then. The next thing we knew, he screamed out loud, "Take it off! Take it off!" What did that man say that for? Some fool turned his stereo up loud, back then we had bumpin' sounds in our cars and his system was pumping that damn song "Billy Jean", and he started thinking he was Michael Jackson. He was pretty good at first 'til he kicked his foot out like Michael Jackson does. His cowboy boot flew in the air and hit a dude right on the top of his head. We were laughing like crazy, but that didn't stop him. I think it even encouraged him some more. He pulled his other boot off and started dancing in his black socks. Yes, he was dancing in his black socks, and it looked like he was doing the forbidden dance. That one guy kept on encouraging him, screaming out, "Take it off! Take it off!" That's exactly what he did with his Michael Jackson style of dancing to the great sounds of "Billy Jean." He was dancing around and pulling his pants down. For some reason, he couldn't get them off. So he put his hands between his legs and grabbed his pants from the other side and looked like a Boston crab. Then he flipped over and did a forward roll. Boy, we were laughing and rolling on the ground. He didn't have anything on but his black socks and his boxers. He started taking them off and his brothers bum-rushed him, trying to tackle him back into their van, but he fought them off and was still trying to dance to "Billy Jean" butt booty naked. His brothers got to chasing after him, and he was still trying to dance while he was running. Then he took off, running down the hill to the highway. There was this Christian family coming down the freeway from a weekend outing, and it was pitch–black outside except for the street lights. He dodged his brothers, and still butt booty naked he jumped right in front of this family's car, and they hit the brakes. All you could do was hear the tires burning on the street, trying to stop. They stopped about an inch in front of him, and he didn't flinch or anything. He was right in between the headlights, and he started dancing like Michael Jackson in front of this Christian family's car – we knew it was a Christian family, they had a cross hanging from their rearview mirror and a Jesus Saves bumper sticker. Remember, it's about two o'clock in the morning. His brothers pulled up on the side of the family's car, grabbed him and threw him in the van, and drove off. You can imagine what was going on in *their* minds.

Right then and there, this became my favorite drug. The baddest drug in the world, that gets you the highest, made for the baddest in the world. That's how I felt, so I stayed wet daddied out. It had really gotten to the point where if it wasn't wet with water, I did not want it. Wet daddies became a balanced part of my daily nutrition. I would go out chasing wet daddies all day long, twelve hours a day it became my job. If you've ever been in the game before, then you know that when you're in the game you feel like you are the baddest, and back then, that's just how I felt.

But people who try to glamorize getting high, they really don't know what they are doing to themselves. With all the getting high on everything that I was getting high on, which was damn near everything, I wasn't about to pass up nothing that came my way. As long as you could roll it up and smoke it, I was with you all the way. The more potent, the more I wanted to hit that good high some more, even if it killed us. Me and my boy's, we could literally watch it kill someone else, and we thought that it was the "bomb good high!" if a drug had you gagging for your very last breath. Afterwards we laughed even while they'd be kickin' on the floor, because we would want to hit it too. That is just how dumb we were. If I knew I was going to live to be this old, and right now I am only forty-seven, I would have taken way better care of myself. Now I have all kinds of health problems from smoking all those drugs. You see, life isn't all about fun. If anyone wants you to get high with them, then they aren't your friend anyway.

A real friend wouldn't have let me suffer the way I am suffering now because of all of my drug use.

God has kept his hand on me for a reason. This is why I know I'm still alive. There's a mission that I know he wants me to complete for him. That's for me to become one of his soldiers and handle the streets in the way that he wants me to—putting all of my life stories together for this book, for other kids to read and learn from my mistakes. It may seem fun at the beginning, but there's pain at the end of the road. Especially if you don't start getting your life straight with God before it's too late. If you don't care enough about yourself, how in the hell do you think someone else is going to care about you? So listen up, homies, don't glamorize any of what you read in this book. If you get the true message of everything that I'm talking about, you'll realize that there's nothing fun about it in the long run. I eventually had to pay for my mistakes the hard way. So be smarter than me and don't learn the hard way. Life is all about choices, so make your choice now before it's too late.

17

ROBBIN' THE HOOD

Now THAT I had discovered how wonderful they were, I started spending all of my time smoking wet daddies. Me and my homies just started coming up with all kinds of stupid things to do. We began to plot up doing burglaries on other people's houses, and that is exactly what we started doing. I remember we did like ten burglaries one morning. We knew the police were hot on our trails, but we didn't care. We just drove around and continued smoking wet daddies and doing burglaries. We didn't know our butts from a hole in the ground. We were damn near robbing houses door to door. It was like we were delivering mail to these people, but taking everything away instead of bringing anything in. We kept firing up wet daddies in their houses while we robbed them, but because we were so high all the time, we got careless and the police started closing in on us. We really should have at least gone to some different locations. But we were so oblivious we didn't even pay attention nor did we care for that matter.

One day we had just finished doing a burglary on this one house and then we went next door to do another burglary. We knocked on the door for about fifteen minutes, you know to check and make sure no one was at home. But I guess the lady was watching us out of her peephole and calling the police at the same time. She just wasn't going to answer the door. We thought no one was at home, so me and my homie decided, "Let's do this." So when we kicked that damn door, man, that steel flew off the hinges and hit the woman in the head. She fell in the middle of the floor and was kicking and screaming. We looked at the woman while we continued to puff on the wet daddies. Then we looked at her again, looked at each other, and said, "Man, this lady is trippin'." We both agreed we didn't want to go on and rob her so we left.

As soon as we got back into the car and drove about two houses down to check out a couple of more houses, about five police cars pulled up, arrested us, and sent us back to jail again. You know, this was beginning to become an all-the-time thing. I began to feel like I deserved to have a private set of keys to my cell because I was there quite often. This was happening to me like clockwork. So as soon as I got out, we were right back to doing the same old routine—smoking those damn daddies and robbin'. I remember going to one house early in the morning while this loving family was asleep. Me and the homies crawled around like snakes on our bellies robbin' this family. We should be all dead to this day because I even crawled into the mother and father's room, sliding around like a snake on my belly.

I slid the rings off that woman's fingers, and I took the husband's watch off his arm without them even waking up. Then I slid right back out of their room without waking them up or even letting them know that we were in their house.

We were very stupid back then, and God had to really be with us. Like always, we ended up back in jail behind all of our ignorance. This last time the judge was getting tired of looking at me. He knew I thought it was all a big joke. So he told me if I ever stepped foot in his courtroom again, he was going to give my black ass twenty years. Believe me, this man was not playing at all.

18

THE BEGINNING OF CHANGE

I TRIED SLOWING my butt down, I was just moving a little too fast for my own damn good. There was this young lady from my neighborhood that I knew. I ended up marrying her and eventually having three kids with her. I thought that married life would slow my behind down.

It did a little, but I was still smoking them damn wet daddies like crazy. Honestly, I got married for all the wrong reasons. Both of our parents told us that we were too young, and we didn't know what marriage was all about. They were all right, we really didn't. I was the one that was really messed up in the head. I can't lie. I was more in love with smoking wet daddies than I was with my wife, and she knew it. She had every right to get away from me. I was really trippin' and carrying her through things no woman should ever have to go through. But that's what happens when your brain is on drugs. I was mostly trying not to get in too much trouble. I was not trying to have to do twenty years. But I still had to try to get my money back on and support my new super huge habit.

That was the damn wet daddies they were the most important thing in my life at the time, so my wife did the smart thing and took the kids and left. But you know, that is what I believe was for the best except for my beautiful kids that were my heart. But they were no compettion, because the drugs just took me under, and I actually didn't know who I was. I had turned into a monster that me and my family didn't even know.

Believe it or not, I loved and still do love my kids unconditionally. But I wasn't the father that I should have been, and right now to this day, this eats me up each and every day. Nowadays I look out toward the sun sets and ask God to bless my three beautiful children. I know one day I'll be able to spend each and every day with them like I've always wanted to. I hope that they will allow me to although I know it can't make up for all the precious years of their lives that I've missed. I wish I had been there to see them growing up and been there for them like I should have. But any time that God will allow me to be with them now is like finding a billion dollars in gold, buried treasure that I've been looking for all my life. Right now, that moment is what keeps me wanting to continue to live for all of my children because they are my everything.

I really wanted to get my life straightened out, but I just didn't know how to get it right because I was still a kid myself. I was just dying for some type of guidance to learn how to be a father and live right. But because of all of these damn drugs, I found myself still acting like a stupid little kid. I started to get pulled back into the streets, and that's just what happened after my wife left me. I got in too deep. The devil was all over my back and was in control of my life.

19

GANG LIFE

A VICIOUS REPETITIVE cycle of drug abuse and gang association is the struggle I was dealing with the first time I met Dr. Joseph Jennings who helped me change my life around. I'll get to him later on in the next few chapters though. One thing I will say on his behalf is he understood the struggle because he was an American Gangster before he became a soldier for Christ. I was the head of a notorious East Spencer Crips street gang in Oklahoma City and affiliated with the worldwide Latin Kings and East Coast Sixty-ninth in South Central Los Angeles as well as Front Hood in Compton. I have always been a very serious type of individual who you really didn't want to cross paths with. I ran about five hundred Crips in Oklahoma City as well as my affiliates in Los Angeles. I was the captain of the ship; whatever missions that were to be carried out were masterminded by me. My homeboy LaMoney was my corporate colonel. I gave him the orders, and he passed it on to Hammerhead and the rest of the crew. LaMoney served a sixteen-year sentence. Hammerhead twenty–five. They both made sure that the rest of the set carried out all the given missions. If anyone failed to fulfill the requirements of their job description, they usually came up missing.

We were running things big time. We had the whole east side of Oklahoma sewed up. No one, including the police wanted to deal with us. We even ran most of the action in the penitentiary and county jail systems. If someone found out you were with East Spencer Crips, no one would mess with you. My homeboys and I would run back and forth between LA and Oklahoma City as well as the East Coast. I set up shop in Oklahoma City and helped the homeboys there get money and respect. I could bring brothers from all over the world if I needed them to handle a situation, and no one would know who they were. So we had it sewed up; the game was on lock.

When I was seventeen years old, I was making around $20,000 a week. I was enjoying life. That was really good money back then. The law picked me up once for questioning concerning three homicides. They claimed to have evidence and witnesses against me for drug trafficking and ordering a hit. They locked me up for a week for investigation. After that first week, they started visiting me at four o'clock in the morning. I was carried down to the broiler room and handcuffed to the heater wall units. I was a young loud talker who did not know how to quit poppin' off at the mouth, but I learned the jail life quickly. About eight huge officers came at me with clubs, and I got the beating that my loving parents never gave me. Despite the fact that I had six fractured ribs and my face resembled that of the elephant man, I wouldn't shut up. I screamed at them, "You could not have done this if I wasn't cuffed to this heater." Then all of a sudden, they all turned around, came back, uncuffed me, and beat my butt again. I knew they were going to kill me. I didn't think I was going to make it through those beatings.

Afterwards, I was thrown in the hole and experienced what is known as being lost in the system. In this situation, the police claimed to have lost all records of you being in jail, especially when someone asks about you. A month had passed and I was still in the hole, butt booty naked. I had a little round hole to crap in, and I was supposed to drink the water that washed it down. I was basically drinking out of the toilet. They gave me doughnuts once a day for thirty days. I lost about fifteen pounds. I had begun to pray to this man my mother always talked about called God.

The next thing I knew after saying that prayer, six hours later, I was being completely released from jail. I never really paid attention to who was allowing me to be released. All I wanted to know was that I was truly getting out of that hellhole. I couldn't wait to hit the streets. LaMoney was there to pick me up and man did we get high. We got high for at least a week nonstop. I don't know how my body held up from all the drugs. There really must have been some serious prayer warriors praying for me. We definitely should have overdosed. We were doing weed, cocaine, PCP, all at the same time, 24/7 for a week.

20

PEACE IN THE HOOD

I WENT BACK to the usual business trying to pick up where I had left off. My homies kept everything rollin'. My little brother Freaked-out Freddy stepped up to hold down the fort. He took over until I was released. I was very impressed. I loved my little brother so much.

He told me some pastor wanted to talk to me. I said, "Some pastor?" And he said, "Yes." I asked him what did a pastor want with me. He said that the pastor only said that he wanted to speak to me. I stayed puzzled for three days when something told me to call him.

His name was Larry Jones from Feed the Children. He had hooked up with Wimpy, a Hispanic gang leader from the south side who ran the south side of Oklahoma, putting it down for the south side. This guy sent for me because everyone knew I was running everything on the east and the west side, where people didn't choose to dwell.

He wanted to set up a meeting with Wimpy and myself. He wanted to have dinner with the two of us. I thought, *Fool, are you crazy? Are you trying to set me up for a hit?* He claimed he only wanted to see if we could come together and through a gang truce, stop some of the killing. It had really gotten off the hook. There was so much going on, and he knew that if Wimpy and I would show solidarity, a lot of it would stop. I told him that it had to be on my terms. I would choose a place I knew was safe. Wimpy could only bring two of his boys, and I'd bring LaMoney, Hammerhead, and my homie Tonto. We met, and Larry started talking all this peace madness. At least, that's what I thought it was at the time. He told us about some rally he was having. I didn't really give a care. But I listened anyway. He wanted to meet again with just me and Wimpy. Wimpy agreed. I guess deep down inside, he wanted to make peace for his people. It wasn't because he was soft or something. He was just tired of all the killing, and he knew that we could both do something to solve it. Someone had to make the first move, and Wimpy saw in my eyes that it wouldn't be me. So he moved first, which really made me respect him. I kept it inside because a real G never shows emotions. I eventually agreed to do it.

We met again, but I still had my boys across the street. I wanted to be on the safe side just in case it got ill. Wimpy came alone. I knew then that he was getting tired of this street life. For the first time, I really listened. We started meeting up again and again. Wimpy and I started to realize we were down for the same cause. We just wanted to help our people and live. We really didn't want all the killings. It just came with the game. We became friends. Larry Jones had brought the Blacks and Mexicans together. We held about six rallies with Larry for a peace treaty. Wimpy and I were together and with that power everyone tripped out, especially when they saw us on TV.

I still hadn't really changed. I would do the rallies and then hit up the hood right afterwards. I had to keep the money flowing. Then they put together this huge rally with people from all over the world. I really didn't care about it. I thought this was a great front for people to think I was doing something different. It might even get the police off my back. In fact, it seemed to make them hotter on my trail.

21

A PASTOR LIKE NO OTHER

The rally was at hand. I wouldn't have gone into that type of atmosphere alone, so I clicked up with twenty of my hoodlums. They rushed Wimpy and me backstage where the cameras were rolling. A lot of rally participants were giving TV interviews.

I noticed a really big guy who was being interviewed. He was staring at me the whole time he was being interviewed. I was the type that didn't back down from anything, so I stared back. As the saying goes, "Game recognize game." Homeboy knew that I was the man running things. Real G's know you don't have to say a word, and this cat knew. After his interview, he walked up to me. My boys jumped up and surrounded him.

He asked if he could pray for me. I asked him what he wanted to pray for me for. He told me that God had a plan for my life. I wondered who the hell he thought he was talking to me this way. He told me that I reminded him of himself when he was my age. I stared at him, mean muggin'. Then I told my boys that it was cool to leave me. I was so puzzled because I had never seen this man before in my life. He had been shot thirteen times and still had about six bullets in his body. I felt everything this guy talked to me about. Then, somehow, I let him pray for me. I was trippin' because it was like my hard shell wasn't so hard anymore. We continued to talk. I found that he'd already experienced everything that I was going through. Then he told me he was a pastor. I laughed. I had never met a pastor like this man in my life. I always thought pastors were people who had never done anything like the things I had done in my life. They always pointed fingers at people like me and my family, and now here's a pastor that's like me.

It was like a fairy tale that I couldn't believe. But it was cool. He made me think that if he could change, maybe there was hope for my life. He told me that he wanted to stay in touch with me because he really cared about me. I said, "Yeah right. How many times have I heard this one before?" But he was the realist pastor or man that I had ever met. So yeah, that's cool I told him. Then I asked him to pray for my boys too. I called them over, and he prayed for them. This guy was all the way down with us.

He asked if we could go out on stage with him. I was like cool, I got your back, and we did. This man walked out into this crowd of sixteen hundred people and told them how it really was. He never bit his tongue about anything he wanted to say, exactly like myself. Something told me inside that this man was now going to be a big part of my life.

When he got ready to leave, he looked me straight in the eye and said, "Tea, I love you, man, and I'm going to call you."

I said, "Cool."

I never thought I would hear from him again. You know how the game goes. But two weeks later, this guy called and said that he's coming down. He wanted to take me and my homies out to dinner. I said, "Cool." This surprised me. Homeboy must have really cared. I was puzzled. This guy started coming around again and again, and calling all the time.

He was like a second father to me now. He was very concerned with everything I was doing and always prayed for me over the phone and whenever he came down. Believe it or not, my "gangsta's life" was changing drastically. I couldn't fight the power of God. I began getting into the music business and trying to get off the streets.

22

MY LA FAMILY

I HOOKED UP with Ice T and his right-hand man, Shaun-E-Shaun, who became a really good friend of mine. They both recognized a true street playa from another part of the world. One thing I can say about both of these two playas from the LA syndicate is that they embraced me and showed me nothing but love. Neither of them had to do that. They could have been just as fake as most of the people in the industry. But they weren't like that. They were really cool and being a true street playa. I'll never forget that. I've always been like an elephant. I never forget anything.

They had a homey who went by the name of O.G. Batman. He was a true LA street playa. He and his little brother, Big Papa, are my true ace's from LA. Batman was one of the original Crips who started the gang back in 1969 with nine other true LA playas. The leader and founder of the Crips, who went by the name Raymond Washington, grew up in the same hood as Batman. Batman was his right-hand man. Wherever you saw Raymond, you saw Batman. They ran LA before Raymond was murdered.

After Batman finally escaped death in the streets and about fifteen years of prison time, Batman decided to change his life around. He's now trying to undo all the destruction that he and his other nine comrades started with the hardcore street gang lifestyle. He spearheaded an organization here in Los Angeles that's run by himself and his beautiful wife, Karen Davis(R.I.P). Their organization goes by the name of "Let's Save the Babies." So Ice T and Shaun told me about OG Batman and what he was trying to do. I said, "Oh yeah. Well, I have an adopted father that is pretty much doing the same thing. So have him get with me and I'll help him get hooked up with my adopted father." They told me if I was to help them with him, they would help me. So I said, "Yeah, well, whatever's clever." If anybody was real, I was the type to help them anyway. That was just how I operated.

Batman called me one day and I think Ice T and Shaun were really still checking me out at the same time. That's just how we operate in the game anyway, and I'm a true playa so that wasn't new to me at all. Me and Bat finally hooked up, and it was like me and his whole family had known each other all of our lives. We got so close that we even started calling each other brothers, and that's just what we all became—family. His wife was just like my flesh and blood sister; he and Big Papa, and everybody else in their family became my family. Whenever I needed anything, they were all there for me. If I ever needed a place to stay, I always had a place to lay my head. You see, in LA, people really have to love you to open their doors to you like that. People keep it real in Los Angeles. If they don't like you, they'll let you know. If they think you are phony and full of it, they'll let you know. If they don't want to have anything to do with you, believe me they'll let you know without any type of hesitation. That's just how it is here in the land of lost scandalous. But these people became my family, and I became theirs. They still watch my back to this day, and I watch theirs. All for one and one for all. I really think me and OG Batman became way closer than Ice and Shaun ever thought we would. Now whenever they see OG Batman, they see Gangsta Tea. That's the way it got, and still is. We are just down like that.

You see, there are real playa's all over the board in every state and every country from all over. Both of us saw this for ourselves. Neither Batman nor myself ever have or will we ever run with fake busta's. We were from different parts of the world but we saw that we were both down and real. We couldn't do anything but become family. After hookin' it up with Batman through Ice T and Shaun–E– Shaun, I became down with the East Coast Crips 6900 Block—the largest Crips gang in Los Angeles. They have my back to this day, and I have theirs.

In truth, I had to hook him up with my adopted dad because I loved Batman, so I knew my dad would love him too. I was seeing some big changes in my life. I had gone from the street life that was into any and every scheme I could think of to someone trying to help others like myself change their ways of living. I knew Batman had grown up dealing with the same things I had, and I wanted to help him find an outlet to change. He wanted to help other people so that he could try and make up for some of the mistakes he had made in his life. It was so unreal to see myself becoming this new person. I knew it was coming from all of the praying Joseph was doing for me. He stayed on top of me just like a father.

I had been moving around for a while, but I eventually made it back to Los Angeles–Compton, California. While I was sitting around one day, the phone rang, and it was Joseph. He said that he was coming in town on business the next day. I told him all about my homeboys Batman and Big Papa. I let him know about their past in the street life and how they were a part of creating the Crips gang back in 1969. They were the walking history of Los Angeles. Their idea had spread all over the US. They had been through and seen a lot of things in their lives, and now they knew it was time to make some positive changes to try and check all the things that had gotten out of control. He told me we could all hook up and do some things. He couldn't wait to meet them.

When he came, he demonstrated his amazing skills as a pastor. He prayed for me and my family, and he was excited to meet the infamous OG Batman. Joseph wasn't new to anything about street life. Because of that, he was able to come in and reach Batman and his family. They recognized that he was real and he meant everything that he said. He prayed for everyone and let them know that he was definitely interested in helping Batman with his organization and anything positive that he wanted to do. He wanted to see all of us using our experience and life stories to help guide the neighborhood kids who didn't have anyone to teach them how to live life the right way. None of us were totally straight, even though we were making some effort to change. But I knew Joseph was serious about getting us involved in some life-changing events. I couldn't get away from what was happening in my life, so I had to submit.

Joseph spent most of his time on the road. He traveled all across the United States and Africa telling his story to America's youth. Joseph had led a very hard life, and he used his story to reach out to young people in their schools and neighborhoods. He wanted Batman and I to come and share our lives with these kids. When we did, we saw what an impact our lives had on them, even teenagers have so many problems nowadays. Hearing about our lives allowed them to open up and really get the message. They were looking for guidance and love, and hearing what we had gone through made them all the more willing to receive God and his plan for their lives.

If it weren't for this man coming into my life, I know that I'd be dead or locked up for the rest of my life. I owe Joseph my life. God sent Joseph to me because he knew I needed a strong father figure to stay on my back. Joseph was my angel sent from God. Because of him I'm living proof that if I can change, anyone can, and that God will definitely put angels in your life to help change you for better. I love my adopted father Joseph Jennings so much for being there for me and opening my eyes to the world. I'm grateful to him for everything he taught me and did for me and my family. R.I.P. Dr Joseph Jennings you will always be remembered.

23

PARTY OVER HERE

AFTER IT ALL, I began to try changing my life around. I started developing Stop the Violence Block Parties in Oklahoma City that were totally off the hook. I became well known for throwing these non- violent block parties, and they were all successful. I had enough street juice so people knew not to come there trippin'. I kept that message going on loud and clear over the DJ's microphone throughout the festivities. We let them all know that anyone who came there and tried to mess up the party for everybody else was going to get their butts kicked by the whole party. That's just what we would've done, and everyone there was down with that. So we didn't have any problems with any of them fools.

The police department and all the newscasters would get mad because the only way they could get there was to fly over with helicopters to film it or take pictures. Otherwise the only other way they could get to where the action was, was to walk two miles to us. That's just how packed all of my events were. The hood loved me like that and supported my block parties. They were the hot spot, and today everybody from the hood still talks about them and wishes I would throw block parties like that again. I was one out of a few that could actually bring peace to the hoods like this.

24

BROTHERLY LOVE

As my life turned around, I had experienced one of the worst tragedies for the very first time in my young adult life. It was concerning my brother Capone who was in the penitentiary again. My brothers were in and out the penitentiaries just like they were taking vacations. That's just how we began to think of them when they took turns going in and out of the joint.

We all knew Capone was also a well-known heroin user, and he shot up behind almost anybody. He believed in sharing his drugs with anybody that wanted some. Heroin users really better think about that because the worst things can happen to you from sharing needles. Me and my brother Tony went with Capone to the doctor to get him a checkup because there were some things happening to his body that he was really concerned about. The doctor asked him if he had ever been tested for the AIDS virus and he said no. The doctor asked if he could test him for the virus and he said, "Okay, that's cool." The doctor ran the tests and said the results would be back in two weeks.

We all went back to the doctor with our brother and got the test results. It said that he had the AIDS virus. I watched the look on my brother's face. It was like his face had turned as white as snow. This disease must have been one of the baddest in the world because I have never seen my brother ever get scared of anything. This thing was the first thing that actually had him scared. I could feel the pain and fear from his eyes. The car was quiet all the way home. You could hear a pin drop. My brother had really changed.

I think my brother really did give up on life that day. He started doing a lot of things that were totally against the law, like he didn't care at all about life anymore. I actually think he wanted somebody to kill him. He didn't want to die from some disease because for him, that would be like dying like a punk, and my brother hated punks. All he knew was that he couldn't die like someone begging for his life. He began to try to see if he could get someone to kill him by doing acts of gangsterism. He just did not care at all. He ended up doing something serious and wound up going to jail again.

My mother and I were the only ones that would go down to court with him for moral support. He had the rest of the family so angry at him for the things that he was doing. My mother and I still stuck beside him and went to court every day that he had court. They eventually ended up giving him two thirty-year sentences side by side. The judge called him a menace to society as he laid his gavel down. Right then and there, me and my mother knew it would be the last time that we would actually see my brother Capone alive as a freeman. This really broke my mother's heart. I hated seeing my mother so torn up like that. It was just too much to deal with. I couldn't help but to shed tears with my mother that day.

They shipped him on out so he could begin doing his time. He survived with the virus for over two years. To get the proper medication, you really have to have some money in order to try to stay alive with it in your system. The good medication is very expensive, and my family just couldn't afford it. After the first two years had gone by, it finally began hitting him and breaking his system down. This was the weirdest, and most deprecating thing I have ever witnessed happening to another human being. My brother was naturally built like he was pumping iron daily and winning fitness contests, but the difference was he never touched a weight. This disease had taken my brother from 250 pounds of pure uncut muscle to a 96-pound bag of bones with skin hanging over it.

They had to ship him over to the penitentiary's hospital because my brother got to the point where he couldn't even walk, and they had to put him on a wheelchair. The doctors there knew he was dying. They told my mother and I that it was just a matter of time. My mother and I knew it too, so we made sure that we went to visit him each and every day. I guess the rest of the family was still mad at him because it seemed like I was the only one who would take my mother to see him each day. I really wanted to be there anyway because no matter what my brother ever did in his life, I still do and always will love him. I really wanted to spend as much time with my brother as I could for the rest of his life. That's just what my mother and I did.

It was like a mission to my mother because, you see, my brother Capone always told us that he was a Zulu. Like Shaka Zulu from the Zulu nations. He always said we were Zulus, and we didn't submit to anything. He always told us he didn't believe in God, and he really meant it. My mother's mission was to convert him from that before he died. Each and every day, we went to his bedside and my mother prayed and prayed for him. She asked God over and over again to have mercy on her baby. My mother prayed at his bedside each day, and prayed so fervently we would remain there until she was literally in tears.

I believe that it was kind of getting to him. I remember one morning when we came to visit him, my mother brought him a mustard seed. She told him that he could move mountains with it if he planted it and let it begin to grow with him. I think my brother took that the wrong way. He knew what she was saying to him, and he took that mustard seed and looked at it really closely in his hand. It seemed like every few hours, he would pick the mustard seed up from the table and look at it for about ten minutes. I began to think that maybe my brother was getting ready to accept God. We knew he was really thinking long and hard about it. When visiting hour was over for that day, he kept his mustard seed on the table next to his bed. When me and my mother came back the next day, the first thing he said was, "Momma, I still got my mustard seed."

Me and my mother looked around the table for it, and we couldn't find it. My mother said, "Son, where is your mustard seed?"

My brother smiled and said, "I planted it like you said."

"I swallowed it."

We laughed and laughed, but I really don't think that was what my mother meant. He began to allow my mother to read the Bible to him after all that fight he had put up against it at first. It was a really huge step for him to let her read him the Bible. She began to do this each and every day, all day long while we visited him at the hospital.

One day, my brother told us that he had a dream, and there was this little drummer man who would not talk to him, but he could talk to the man through his mind like ESP. He said the man would respond by just a nod of his head and a wave his hands for Capone to follow him. So my brother said that he followed him to this village, and my brother said that he kept asking him, "Hey, little man, where are you taking me?" The little man would just wave his hand telling him to come on, and my brother said, "Hey, little man, I am tired of walking, where are we going?" And my brother said, "I am not walking no more." Then he said that the little man kept waving his hand saying, "Come on." He said he stopped walking and the little man waved his hand, and everything started shaking hard like an earthquake. My brother said, "Okay, man, I am coming, I am coming." Then my brother told us they eventually came to the little village, and it looked like all the houses were all burned up and it was all black and smoked out on the side that they were standing on. He said that there was a river stream that ran in front of this smoked-out village. Then my brother said, "Hey, little man, I don't like it here. I want to go back." He said the little man shook his head no, and my brother said he kept telling him that he wanted to go back, but the little man shook his head no again.

Then my brother said he looked across the river stream, and he saw his grandmother and his auntie. Then he said, "Hey, little man, I want to go over there. That is my grandmother and my aunt and some of my uncles. I want to go over there, little man. I want to go over there."

The little man shook his head no again, and he asked him again, "Why can't I go over there, little man, Why?" He said to my brother in his mind, *The ticket machine will let you know if you can go over there.* He told him that it would print out all the bad things that my brother had done in his life, and if he was under the requirement list, he could go over there. So the little man turned on the machine that was strapped around his chest like a drum. Man, my brother said that machine started lighting up like crazy. It was printing out stuff like it couldn't stop. My brother said, "Hey, little drummer man, didn't I ever do anything right?" And the machine continued to go crazy. It just wouldn't stop at all. So the little drummer man pointed down at the smoked-out village, and my brother said, "No, little man, no." Then my brother said that his grandmother, aunts, and his uncles all disappeared, and the little man told him that he would be back to get him again—to bring him back to the smoked out village.

My brother said he woke up, but even when he was wide awake, he would tell us when the little man was in the room. Sometimes he would be scared to talk when the little man was in the room. Right then and there, me and my mother knew that it wouldn't be long before we were going to lose him. My mother really began praying out loud for my brother, and my mother is like a prayer warrior. She knew she had to get him to accept God quickly, and she knew she didn't have much time to make this happen. She began to try everything in her power that she could do and then some. Believe it or not, that evening my brother began asking my mother about God, and she had the answers for him. He would smile so happily as visiting hours began to come to an end. My mother asked my brother if she could pray for him, and my brother actually told her yes. He even bowed his head; we both did while my mother prayed for him. We both kissed my brother and told him how much we loved him, not even knowing that this was the last time that we would be kissing him and telling him that we loved him while he was alive. We both said afterwards that something felt different this time as we left. I carried my mother home, and I told her I loved her and I'd see her tomorrow when I picked her up so we could go and visit my brother.

I got a call from my mother at four thirty that morning. She said, "Terry, baby, your brother has left us." My mother and I shed tears over the phone. All I began to wonder was if my brother decided to submit and ask God for forgiveness for all of his sins. We still don't know to this day if he did or not. All I can say is that my mother worked on him up until the very last minute of his life. This was the first time I really began to learn how serious death was. Death is the baddest pimp in the world. There is no way you can defeat him. It doesn't matter how bad you think you are, he will defeat you. My brothers and I have carried so many mothers and families through so much pain. You never really know or understand it until it happens to you and yours. So now I know that you have to respect life and death because it is really much more serious than most kids could ever imagine. Most of them try to talk all that hard street talk, but they have never had to really respect it yet. They have never dealt with anything as serious as the death of someone very close to them. Once they do, they will truly understand it unless they are just plain stupid. In that case, they won't survive long any way.

25

MARRIED LIFE

R IGHT BEFORE CAPONE passed away was around the time that I met the beautiful young lady whom I'm married to now. She also had three kids of her own when I met her. I guess you can say we're like The Brady Bunch. She had three kids, I had three kids, and now we have one together. She was a person that had dreams like I did. She was trying to get some things going on for herself like developing a modeling company. You can say we both had some of the same dreams of having our own businesses. She was a real go–getter, and I was too. I know this is what really attracted me to her. We were on the same page, and we were trying to follow our dreams. So we started working together on making some of our dreams come true.

Melinda started hosting my block party shows for me. We had over one hundred raw but talented rap groups, and every time we had a show, all the rappers, singers, etc., tried to be a part of our shows. That's how dope they were. We even began to develop our own Hip Hop Music Video TV show that was aired on public access channels. We began to turn heads from a lot of well-known, big-time record labels that wanted us to help them support their artists. But we really didn't have the money to continue doing the show. I think God wanted us to learn more about the business end of things first. So we had to pull the plug on it and everyone was really disappointed. A lot of people loved the show. We also had a few labels that were talking about giving us a budget to continue but we were dealing with a lot of other things and trying to decide if we were going to become a family or not. Whenever you try to develop a family with kids coming from both parents, it's a difficult task. That's exactly what it was, and it was very rough. None of us could see eye to eye. My future wife and her kids saw the world one way, and me and my children saw it another way. None of us were trying to bow down. Still to this day, I can't believe that I'm still married to my wife. We seemed like we just couldn't get along. But this time, I can actually say that I really love my wife. I understand what a marriage is about now. I guess like the saying, "What goes around comes around." This is like payback for everything I put my first wife through. I'm really trying to hang in there.

I really think God put me in my wife's life to help her raise her daugthers. I feel like my wife had really been through a lot in her life. She was abused by men and even some of her very own family members, and she was trying so hard to overcome all of that abuse when we met. Her wonderful children somehow got caught up in the middle of it all, just like mine did in my first marriage. The children are always the ones that have to pay for their parents' sins. I made a promise to God that I'll never walk away from any of my kids as long as I live, if God will give me the opportunity to make it up to my other three. I guess God was holding me to all of that because Melinda's three children are just like my very own. I don't even look at them as if they have another father. In my eyes, I'm their father; that's just how much I've grown to love them. No one can tell me any different. We do have one child together as well, so I could never leave these four children of mine. I guess you can say Gangsta has seven kids and they are all mine. That's just how it is. All seven of them mean the world to me, and they are what I live for now.

Now I have something of my own in this life to live for and to set morals and values. I try to teach my children not to make any of the mistakes I've made in life. I know it's going to be a lot of work for me because I am still in need of God's help myself. I have been drug free for fifteen years now. I'm really trying to be a father to all of my kids. The one thing that I have learned to do for my children is to tell them all the truth about life. I tell them the truth about me, and I use myself as a guinea pig and an example to let them know that I've been there. I learned the hard way so I don't want them going that route. Doing this has really kept my two older daughters' heads on straight. It makes me so proud because I feel like I've done the right things in raising them. Especially for being a person that is miles and miles away from being perfect or having my own life straightened out completely.

To this day, the streets still call me to go out and do dirt. I think about my kids in Oklahoma and my wonderful kids with me here. They help me hang in there and keep my head up. Sometimes my daughters know what I'm thinking, and they just come up to me and tell me, "Daddy, you know you have done so much for us, we would like to just tell you that we love you so much and we need you." That knocks all the criminal thoughts right out of my mind and let's me know that God works in mysterious ways. Nothing would ever have stopped me like that before. But now I've run up against something that God made called love. I found out that's one thing I wasn't stronger than.

I'm so glad that God has blessed me with this. Maybe that's a part of something that my wife and I needed because we probably both didn't get all the love we truly deserved as young children. I have really come to the place where I'm searching for nothing but peace in my life. I'm so tired of negative and headache drama. We argue and fuss a lot, but we don't hit or fight at all. Of all the dirt I have done in my life, my father always taught us never to hit a woman and always respect our elders. Through everything I've ever done, I still and always will respect women and my elders. So I don't hit women. I don't even like to fuss or argue with them.

So really, I'm praying for me and my wife to get over that hump. Most people don't believe we've been together as long as we have. Whether someone is around or not, we are usually at it. This really isn't good for us or our children. To me, it's beginning to affect our children. I really don't want that because I love them so much. I don't want any destruction to happen to them. So I'm really hoping and praying for me and my wife to get it together. I really and truly love her so much. You see, to me, my wife is my best friend. Anyone that really knows me will tell you I don't trust people at all and I don't consider many people my friends. You have to be someone that's really been there for me, before I'll call you a friend. I just don't do that. I have many adversaries but very few close friends. That's just how it is with me. My wife, to me, is my best friend. I would give her my right or left hand if it came down to it. I believe she'd really do the same for me because of everything we have been through, we are still together, and we've been through some real dilemmas.

I remember times when we had to push around a shopping cart to fend for our family because we didn't have a car. We used the shopping cart as our car to go to the laundry mat, to go to the store. We carried a shopping cart from the store and walked our groceries back home in the cart. That's how it was for awhile. In the neighborhood, it wasn't a big deal because all of the homeless homies pushed a shopping cart. Now I was pushing one too, and it was cool with me.

I started really getting cool with it. I began to kind of look forward to pushing my shopping cart daily. I began to meet some of the other homeless guys up on the corner, and we began to meet there almost every morning and talk. I found out that they were really some pretty cool cats. I started to enjoy hanging with them in the mornings. The only problem was that I wasn't homeless, I just didn't have a car. They didn't hold that against me. They said I fit right in with everybody else because I never acted as if I was better than them.

I treated them like they were all human beings; that we're just dealing with some hard times. People can be so cruel and mean to other human beings just because they're homeless. I really hate that, and maybe because I was so poor all my life, I could really understand and relate to them.

After my wife started to see how I began to not want to go anywhere without my shopping cart, she said we are getting a car. She felt like I was beginning to like pushing my shopping cart just a little too much. She didn't want me to fall into that kind of a slump. So we eventually did just what my wife said, we got a car. I didn't forget about my new found friends or the way they were living.

If I ever get in a better financial position, my goal is to assist in developing some types of programs to help end homelessness. I feel like no one should ever have to live like that.

26

THE STRUGGLE

MY WIFE IS always looking out, even when I think she isn't. I remember when we actually got kicked out of that same home and they gave us five days to move out. This was really a trip man. You're talking about a family bonding, and sticking together to pull through it. We didn't have anybody there for us, but a woman that we had met from church. She opened her home for us and allowed us to stay at her house until we could get another place. This is a woman who is used to having her nice condo all to herself. When she saw that we were in need, she let all six of us move in and made everything that was hers ours.

No one else tried to help us at all. Not even the rest of the people from the church congregation that we attended. Not one of the men offered to help us move our things out of the house or anything. So much for a church family right? That is just how people are, as long as they are getting tithe's, and your volunteer services, they'll go Jesus crazy in your corner, but when their so-called brother in Christ really needs them, they always seem to turn their backs. They all did except the one lady that opened her house to us. She was a blessing to us, and I'll never forget her.

But it seemed like we meant nothing to the rest of the church, even though we were there every Sunday and paid our tithes like clockwork. As long as we were doing that, all we heard was Jesus talk and God bless you. But when a brother fell into need and needed a hand, they turned their backs. Me, my daughters, and my wife, moved all of our things out of the house by the grace of God. We are talking three bedrooms, a living room, and kitchen full of furniture and appliances that were really too heavy for women to be trying to pick up. We were all we had, and we did it together. We know how to come together when we need to.

Now we were homeless like my fellow comrades, and I began to pray then. God, please just let me get a home for my children. I felt so little. I found out a new pain. That pain is when you have a two-year-old son, a five-year-old son, a fourteen-year-old daughter, and a sixteen-year-old daughter, and their little eyes look at you, and you have to tell them they no longer have a home. Man, this was worse to me than shooting yourself in the head with a gun. I was supposed to be a man, and I just kept on wondering how in the hell did this happen. It was just a good thing because through all that, God still worked through the lady from church and didn't allow my children to have to actually live in the street. We began to pray as a family and thank God for that each and every day.

Like that old saying, "When it rains, it pours." Then all of a sudden, I found out that back home, my brother-in-law had been missing prior to this. They found him in an abandoned house. He was shot up with some strychnine poison, hung from the rafters of the house, and left there while his body had fully deteriorated. This boy was just like my flesh-and-blood brother. He was my sister's husband and my niece's father. I felt so bad that I was too poor to be there with my family through those times. I wouldn't let them know what me and my family were going through at the same time. It was just too much, and I figured God would help us.

Then all of a sudden, some guys blew my nephew's brains out with a 0.44 handgun and tried to throw his body in his mother's yard. These fools were so dumb that they picked the house two houses down. This was really too much. I was homeless and dealing with two deaths. I really began to fall into a very deep depression because I loved my brother-in-law and my nephew so much. I began to really want revenge, but I was just too poor to do anything, and I had a wife and kids that I had to get situated. I know this was truly a way to keep me from going to get revenge because everyone in my family was scared. I was going to come home and do just that. They knew how I was.

27

FREAKED-OUT FRED

To REALLY PUT the icing on the cake, I got another phone call from my brother Boo-da-man. He began to seem more and more like like the grim reaper with each recurring call I received from him. I love my brother Boo-da, but every time he called, it was getting to be nothing but bad news. I didn't want to hear from him again like that, but he was calling again. He told me they had killed little Fred.

I said, "What?"

He said, "Man, they killed little Fred."

"Man, quit playing like that."

"Man, you know, I don't play like that."

My whole body just went numb, and I was speechless. Now these fools had gone too far. It was like the devil was trying to destroy me. He knew what he was doing because this was my little brother. This was like shooting me straight through the heart with a bow and arrow.

I just dropped the phone. To me, it was like the end of the world. I just couldn't believe what was happening back to back to back, and now a backbreaker. I was just too weak after that hit. It was like the devil had sunk my battleship. I loved this little curly headed boy whom I had raised all my life. Now he was gone and brutally murdered. He was shot seven times with a high-powered rifle. I just kept saying over and over again, "They aren't going to get away with this. They aren't going to get away with this." It felt like the devil had just ripped my heart right out of my body, and kept me alive to suffer through it.

My dad started talking to me on the phone, and I was crying on the phone while I was talking to him. Daddy said, "Terry…listen to me, son, Fred is gone now. There is nothing you can do for him now but pray for him. Son, I do not want you to come here. Stay where you are." The reason my father was telling me this was that he knew how much I was hurting. He felt it. He knew I was going to come there and get myself in some serious trouble. My daddy made me promise him that if I came there, I would only come to the funeral. He would carry me back to the airport and put me back on the plane. I said, "Okay, Dad. I have to say good-bye to my little brother. I promise." My dad wouldn't let me too far out of his sight because he knew me. My entire life I've been known as the one who makes things happen. Nobody wanted to get on my bad side. I wasn't a tough guy, but I didn't take crap off anybody either. People knew that if you ever took one of mine, you were losin' all of yours. That's who I always was. No questions asked. The situation just got handled.

As hard as it was for me, I stuck to my promise. He just didn't want to lose another son, and I could understand that. I love him for all of that. Fred's funeral was one of the hardest things I have ever had to deal with it seemed in all of my life. I felt like life is filled with nothing but pain. Fred was my baby brother. I watched him grow up. He was my life. I couldn't believe that he wasn't with me anymore. I was never going to see him again.

Lucky I still had my own family to come back to. These were some of the hardest days I've ever had to deal with in all of my life. I never ever thought I could get over that hump, and believe it or not, I'm still dealing with it. I don't think I'll ever get over my little brother's death. It still hurts to this day. I have just been dealing with the pain day by day. My children give me the love and the will to continue. That's the real reason why I'm still here now and I know it.

28

LIFE TODAY

W E EVENTUALLY GOT another apartment. God pulled us through another ordeal without the devil totally destroying us. I know God is really looking out for us because if he wasn't, I would have given up on it all because I'm still trying to get over that emotional hump. I'm really trying to get a new start in life so I can try to take care of my family financially. I'm forty-seven years old, and I didn't go to college. Hell I didn't even graduate from high school. All I had to fall back on was the streets.

My body suffers from all the drugs that I've abused it with. There is a lot that I didn't understand then, but looking back at everything I've done and experienced in my life, I have a lot of regret. I know that I had the potential to do great things for myself and others. But my situations prevented me from seeing what was really in front of me. It's hard to see that silver lining when you're surrounded by dark clouds and floods. It's hard to imagine that there's a heaven or that you can ever make it there when you're surrounded by demons and hell. I couldn't open my eyes and see past my anger and pain to realize what God had given me. Today, I try to spend every moment of my life doing just that and appreciating the fact that he brought me this far.

I believe my blessings are going to come through my music. I can tell a lot of stories about a lot of my life experiences and maybe help some other kids that may be going through what I've been through. That's my plan. It seems like the only thing I really have to take care of is my family. I want to put my kids through college because I don't see any other way unless I go back to the dope game. God knows I'm willing to take care of my kids by any means necessary. God also knows I'm really trying to live right. I don't ever want to go back into doing anything that's not right in God's eyes, or my children's eyes. They are who I live for. I know God is going to bless me through my music without a doubt.

As for me and my wife, I truly believe she deserves much more than me. I'm not the man she truly loves. We had a lot in common when we met, but we are definitely two ships sailing from two countries on opposite sides of the world. I'm nowhere near the type of person that she is accustomed to being with. She's used to the classy, educated type which is the total opposite of a street hustler like me. She married me because she knows I truly love all of her children and treat them as if they are my very own. Men like that are really hard to find. I don't feel that someone like myself can give her the happiness that she needs. I can feel it in my heart. Her heart is elsewhere, and no one should ever settle for something that they don't sincerely want, under any circumstances. But I'm not trippin'. If her heart is somewhere else, then I guess her heart is somewhere else.

My life is all about my kids right now, and they are who I live for. Me and my wife may not see eye to eye because we are from totally different worlds. With all that we have been through together, I could never turn my back on her. She will always be like a real good friend to me. To be honest, through all this mess she is still my best friend, compared to the fakers that I have called that ironically tragic word friend just to turn around and get stabbed in the back by them. I just hope one day she is truly blessed with everything she expects out of life. I hate that I'm not the man that can fulfill all of her dreams. I just wish I was the man that she truly loved. But I'm not and that's that. I will always love her anyway no matter what happens between us. It's like this, if it's meant to be, then we will be. If it's not meant to be, God will send us in totally different directions. I will always love her no matter what. I will never forget our memories. She will always have a place in my heart no matter what cards I'm dealt in the future. I'll put most of my focus into being a dad and loving my children unconditionally. The rest of my time is for my music career.

29

RAPPIN' IN LA

I HAD HOOKED up with Ice T and Shaun-E-Shaun. Me and Ice T started work on a song called the "Realist." We finally completed the song in a studio in Hollywood. It is still yet to be released. I'm still trying to get something going on now. I also started another project with a cowboy by the name of MC Wild Turkey. We were introduced by the producer that did the final mixing for the "Realist." He was from Arkansas and I was from Oklahoma. It seems like everybody from the South can relate so we ended up producing music together. He had created this unique musical genre that consists of country and western music, mixed up with hip-hop/alternative/pop/rhythm and blues. This music was everything rolled up into one. To top it off, he was a for real cowboy and a full-fledged country boy.

The producer thought that it would be so cool for this guy to do a song with one of Ice T's boys. He asked me to listen to this guy's music and let him know what I thought about it. He gave me a picture of the guy, and I thought he looked just like the Marlboro man from the billboards. I listened to the guy's music, and I laughed and laughed because I knew the world wasn't ready for this. It was such a new fusion of music. This would definitely be making music history. Hip-hop, country, and western had never been done in music, and this was the first.

Believe it or not, this music was dope. It was really good. I knew this was a project that wasn't going to be easy to bring out, but when we did get it out there, it would take over because it would be something completely new and historical. So I called the producer and told him, "Hell yeah, I'm with this project." I really don't think to this day that producer knew I was from the country too and right next to Arkansas. So I told him to set the meeting up.

When I walked into that room, I didn't know what to expect. One thing I can say, I really didn't expect what happened. I was so used to serious racism from any white person coming from the south and especially coming from that area. You know, I did not tolerate that type of mess anyway. So I really didn't have any type of idea on how this meeting would go. But you know, God works in mysterious ways. I walked into that room wondering if I was going to have to deal with that, but it was totally different. That damn Wild Turkey was really a cool man. That brother embraced me and we began talking.

It was just like we knew each other for years. We hit it off, right off the bat. We even had better chemistry together than he and his producer. I think the producer began to get jealous. Me and Wild Turkey began to get closer and closer, and the producer didn't like that. His real plans were to take over Turkey's project and make all the money for himself. He was really trying to take advantage of Wild Turkey, keeping me away from him. He knew I had learned the business very well, but Turkey on the other hand didn't know the business and how cutthroat Hollywood was. But Turkey was a really nice kid and I saw that.

I knew what his producer was up to, but the LA code is, you don't get into anyone's business. So I tried to stay out of their business. But Turkey constantly wanted to do more work with me. The producer was trying to keep it down to a minimum, and he was really getting disturbed by that. Greed is one of the seven deadly sins. He also didn't want me to reveal to Turkey what was actually going on. I stayed out of it, but I was beginning to get mad because now the racism that I thought I was going to be getting from Wild Turkey was coming from the producer. I don't play that, and I told them just like this, "Okay, if I am going to keep having to deal with all this, I want everything to be split fifty-fifty." I wanted full partnership of the Southern Rap Commission. I let them know I'm not with all this stupidty. I have a family to take care of, and I don't have time for the madness. So either I'm a full-fledged partner or I'm hitting the highway. I didn't need it, and I was sick of seeing this nice kid being taken advantage of.

It seemed like every time I made an effort to change my life around, the devil was everywhere. But God stayed on my side and told me to let Turkey know what was going on because this kid had a really good heart, and God's children should never be taken advantage of like this. This was crazy. So I called Turkey up and had him to come over my house, and we drank beer and talked. I told him everything that I saw going on and educated him on a lot of things he didn't know about the business and the people here in Los Angeles. This kid really played sponge that day and paid close attention. He sat back for a week and started really seeing what was going on. It was like there was a new Marshal in town. He saw for himself that he had a deadly snake in his camp that really didn't give a damn about him at all.

Boy did Turkey start cleaning house. That boy made me an equal partner and, boy, did that producer get mad. And Turkey told him this was his thing, and if he wanted to pull the plug on his thing, then there wouldn't be anymore Southern Rap Commission. This was just a producer. Since when has a producer ever been a part of a group? Boy, was this guy pissed. Turkey even got to the point to where he felt he couldn't trust this guy anymore, and he asked the guy for the ADAT tapes that we had recorded the album on. Turkey had paid the guy over twenty-five thousand dollars for everything, including for him to engineer, etc. And this guy wouldn't give him his ADAT tapes. He even had the nerves to say he felt like he was one of the artists, and he had to get in the middle of this because it was just too much for me and Turkey.

I began to start looking at Turkey as one of my little brothers who needed my help from a big bully. I said to the producer, "Man, you must be joking, right? Where are you on any of this album? If you can show me one place then I'll believe you are one of the artists." He knew he wasn't on this album at all, and he also knew that he had been paid for his services, but he just didn't want to let that boy's tapes go. He called himself punking him out. I asked him right in front of Turkey.

I said, "Do you think Turkey is a punk or something?"

He hesitated and said, "No, but I just feel like I am one of the artists."

"Man, we just went through all that already. Man, the gig is up. You're busted. Give the boy his ADATS."

He had agreed he was going to give them to him the next day, but I knew that was only because I was there. He was fronting. That next day came, he was giving Turkey all kind of grief and told him he wasn't going to give him his tapes. So Turkey called me and told me what was going on. This just pissed me off, so I called him up and I said, "What is the deal now, man?" He started poppin' off some more type of crap. I said, "Hey, man, look here. I am tired of playing these games. I want you to get all of my ADAT tapes that I have done up there, and I want you to drop them off at Turkey's job. I want his too, or we are going to have some serious problems."

This producer knew I meant business when I told him that because he knew I was well connected all over South Central Los Angeles, and I was not the one to play with. Do you know he had all of our tapes over there within twenty minutes. That was the end of all that drama.

To this day right now Wild Turkey and myself have been the Southern Rap Commission. This kid became a great little brother to me. My other little brother was killed so I've adopted Turkey, and I watched over him like a large chicken hawk and would kick his butt when I had to. We let each other know when we think the other is slipping. We argue up a storm just like brothers, so I think that's what makes us so unique. We stand together totally and watch each other's backs. We put God first, our family's second, and everything else like business afterwards. So with a strong foundation like that, I really don't think we can be stopped. We are just waiting our turn to get our shot, and with all of God's blessings and from where we have come, God has let us know we are well on our way.

30

LA 2000

MAN, THEY SAY the streets here in South Central Los Angeles haven't been this sick since 1987. This gang activity is so out of hand. It's ridiculous.

The police force pulled our gang task force units because of the LA police scandals. So I guess they call themselves making the people pay by allowing us to be robbed and murdered. It's to the point where you can't even walk down the street in broad daylight without being shot at or killed.

It's like Martial law. Nobody here likes anybody, and it's like everybody wants to kill you. It feels kind of like a World War, like you're living in the trenches. I feel like I should be a colonel by now. We're having about ten gang murders each and every night, just in South Central alone. We aren't even counting the other cities here in Los Angeles where most of these crimes are happening in broad daylight. Little kids trying to play and enjoy life are getting shot off their bikes. Toddlers are being shot off their big wheels, and grandmothers are being shot in their kitchens baking cookies for their grandkids.

You can't even drive down the street without being hit up by other gangs. If you know what's best for you, I suggest you hit the gas and get out of their hood. If you don't, nine times out of ten they are on their way to hit you up again. The next time, they're going to let their gun talk to you. You can't even walk to the store to buy some butter and milk, minding your own business without all this madness creeping up on you. So what are you supposed to do when you are trying to raise a family and live right? I was always taught here in Los Angeles, "It's an eye for an eye." That's the G-code on the streets. You take one of mine, I'm taking all of yours, and we don't give a damn. That's just how it is and these fools enjoy killing you. To them, it is better than sex. This is their way of getting their rocks off. This is why I go to the track and run three miles a day. Here, you better be in some kind of shape, because I don't care how bad you may think you are, these hood G's will pull your trump card. If you like breathing, you'd better have some kind of track game and be able to jump fences and run down allies at a high speed. The strong survive here and every G living in the streets of LA thinks he's the baddest. These fools will lay you down because we see it on a daily.

Sometimes I sit back and think why am I here? This place is like an indoor/outdoor penitentiary. All day long, the police helicopter is always chasing somebody. It's gotten to the point where I can't even go to sleep without hearing sounds of gunshots and helicopters so close it's almost like they're landing on top of my apartment. I've grown so used to the spotlights shining through my bedroom window I almost feel neglected and find it difficult to sleep at night. Me and my children get up every morning with the expectation that there will be a high speed chase on the news, and we watch to see if the bank robbers will outrun the LA police department for entertainment. It's so sick that sometimes we catch ourselves cheering on the bank robbers to get away.

I really feel like this isn't appropriate for my children, but there's no such thing as Barney's world here in Los Angeles. They don't have time to grow up as kids. They have to be like adults here and learn to roll out of bed and hit the floor to escape another drive by. Many of these kids don't make it. You can't even sit in your own home and watch television with your family, without these fools kicking in your door while you and your family are watching cartoons. They do a home invasion on you and your family and take the television with the cartoons on it and everything else you own. Sometimes you and your children become casualties. You have to really pay close attention to who knocks on your door. In all actuality, you can't really answer your door without a pistol, because these fools will still blast on you.

I remember when you used to be able to say hi to people. You say hi to a person nowadays here in Los Angeles, they start trippin' when you're only trying to be nice. They sit around telling their homies, "Ah dog, that fool is trippin'. That punk said hi to me like he knows me.

"That fool doesn't know me like that. Let's go serve that fool because he must think I am soft or something. Cuz, he's fixing to get smoked." That's just what they will do; shoot you over something dumb like that.

That 'loop-loop' is a drug that is driving these little gang bangers nuts here. They just can't handle it. I just try to look out for my family, keep them all alive, and hope one day I can get them far away from all of this. I pray every day for my family's safety and for God to give me the strength to continue to be able to protect them and make a way to make it better for them. I have seven beautiful, wonderful kids and a beautiful wife. I'm an ex-gangbanger, drug dealer, and drug abuser that should have and many times could have accidentally overdosed and checked out for good.

All I have in life is my family. I have a son that is getting ready to go to college, and I don't know how I'm going to send him, all I know is that, we don't have any money for it, and I don't see where it will come from except for God blessing us with the money from somewhere. My son is an excellent student and football athlete who run's a 4.4- God has told him and myself that he will attend a great university and graduate to play in the NFL. So I must follow God's word and have the faith that these doors will open by the year 2016, and I will be able to pay for him to attend. There is no doubt in my mind that somehow this will happen. If I don't have anything else in this world, I do have faith in God. In my heart, I will make this happen by any means necessary. I will do anything for my children, and if I can't achieve it, then I feel I need to be locked up for the rest of my life or dead. To me, that's a useless man, and I can't go out like that.

Where do I go from here? I absolutely don't have any other hope of a future besides my music career, otherwise the only thing left in the game for me to do would be to stack up the type of capital that I'm going to need that fast by selling drugs again. So were do I go from here? I will be damned if I grow old homeless and pushing on a shopping cart. Not being able to make ends meet for my family is something I refuse to go through ever again.

Man, I really feel like my family has suffered enough behind all my mess. Sometimes, I feel ashamed to even think about calling myself a man. I could never fill my father's shoes, and to me, that's the worst feeling in the world because that really means a lot to me. So I have to get to the point where I can at least say I'm taking care of my children and my wife like I am supposed to. That means the world to me.

We all know how reality is for an ex-con, ex-gangbanger, ex-drug addict, ex-drug dealer, ex-robber, ex-hustler, and everything else I've done in my life, so who's really going to give a guy like this a job or an opportunity? Let's keep it real, it's not going to happen. When people see me—a large, bald-headed man with tattoos, society gets scared. I deal with this on a daily basis. But right now my faith is strong and I believe God will take care of all my children and my wife. I don't need anything for myself, except what's needed for my family. That's all I need to make me happy.

At this point in my life, I am trying to be the best father that I can possibly be. My children and I know that I have a lot of issues that I'm still dealing with from when I was a child myself. But we all try to keep everything on the table. I don't lie to my kids about anything, and I believe that's why we have such a great relationship now. We can be friends as well as family, and we can also talk about almost anything together. That really makes me feel good inside. It lets me know I'm doing my job. My wife and I really want a loving family so that's one thing we can both agree on right now without a doubt. Who knows, through God, I believe in time we may be able to agree on other things as well. I really love this woman, and I hope I can also be the man of her dreams. Everything can happen through Jesus's name, and I have the faith on that as well.

I'm trying so hard to stay on the right path, but a lot of times, I feel like giving up. I can't lie. But I look down at those little faces, and they are the ones that really keep me in the game. I want to make it to the light. Once this ghetto darkness gets a hold of your life, believe me, it doesn't want to let you go. It will continuously try to chain you up and keep you there. But God will put people in your life to keep hope alive for you, and it's still not going to be easy. Listen to me when I say this, the ghetto darkness wants to do nothing but distinguish your fire and keep you close to the gates of hell. But if you look ahead through the fog, you will always see a glimpse of the light and that's God's way of letting you know there's still a chance for you. The decision is yours and no task in life is easy. I feel like I have been to hell and back. Now my body is all broken down because of the banged-up life that I've allowed myself to live. I have been there, and all I can say to the next man is, you do not want to be there and go through what I have had to live with, especially if you don't have to. Life is all about choices, so you make the choice of what you want to do. I won't tell you what is right or wrong, but read this book and you can choose where you're going. I've lived on the darkside all my life. I don't like it and don't want it anymore.

I want to try my chances getting to the light. I know I'm not even close to being there yet because the devil and God are still playing tug-of-war with my life. I am trying very hard to go to God's side because that's where I want to be now. I'm sick of that ghetto darkness, and I want to be in the light. I ask myself this every day, "Where do I go from here?"

31

PEACE OUT

To God the Almighty for all the blessings he has given me and for just being there for me at all times. I am trying so hard. Father God, please don't give up on me.

Special thanks to my beautiful goddess wife, there is no way that I could have done this without you, My most precious Melinda Bernadette Carney. You are my strength. You keep me flowing like Niagara Falls. You are the air that I breathe, my life, my darling. I love you more than you can ever imagine. I look forward to spending the rest of our lives together, forever always and until eternity.

To Howard and Mary Carney, I love you so much you both couldn't imagine. One day, I hope I can make you proud of me. To my adopted father Dr. Joseph Jennings, man, I owe you so much. I love you man. I never thought you would still be there for me, and I feel you are. I really don't know how I can ever thank you. You are my guardian angel. I know if you wouldn't have stayed on me the way you did, I would be like all the rest of the guys I was running with; locked up in the penitentiary for life or buried in the cemetery. I want to also thank a third father to me, and that is Elwood Slade for just being there and talking us street homies out of a lot of the ill things that we knew we shouldn't have done and letting us know what was right. Thank you so much. For that beautiful wife of mine, I really want to give you a very big thank you for putting up with all my crap. I know I'm not the type of man that you deserve, but I hope one day I can give you the lifestyle you are worthy of. It has been twenty-two long years of nothing but hard and crazy times, but you have been there even though you did not have to. So I guess what I'm trying to say to you is that I love you so much. Even if you feel like I don't appreciate you, I really do, and I even admire you for sticking by my side through it all. I will always have nothing but love for you and as long as God gives me life, I will always be there for you. I love you, girl. To all seven of my children I love you so much. You are my world and my everything, words just cannot tell you all how I feel about each and everyone of you. Bunnie M. Poullard, Opal S. Poullard, Terry C. Carney Jr, Marcus D. Carney, Giovonni D. Sanchez, Brittany A Carney, and Lawon D. Carney, I love you all so much, and God is going to continue to make it better for all of us. If you do get a hold of this book, please don't ever do any of the things your father has done. Stay children of God, stick with the light because there is no future in that ghetto darkness. Daddy loves you all so much. To all my sisters and my brothers, Harold G. Carney, Ruby Jean Carney, Jamal Bey Johnson (Little Johnny is what we call him), and Hot Rod Carney, I love you. Clinton Ray Johnson Jr (Capone), rest in peace, man. I miss you so much. I love you and wish you were here to help me with a lot of this stuff. You know, sometimes it feels like you are there guiding me because I am trying to do everything that you used to preach to us about regarding business. I feel like it is you working through me for the family. So if it is, I just want to say thank you and I love you so much, my brother. You will never be forgotten. My sister, Darlene, I know I don't talk to you much, but I love you so much too, so smile; to my sisters Reta and RIP El. What can I say, you girls know that you hold a special spot in my heart; you mean the world to me too and don't you ever forget that. RIP Bruce, and to my brother Curtis, you look for the light and get your head on straight. Don't let the enemy steal your glory. I love you, both get it right. Tony and Shirley, I love you guys, keep an eye out on Dad for me. If you need anything, let me know. To my little brother, Fredrick L. Smith a.k.a. Freaked-out Freddy, boy, God knows there is not a day that goes by that I don't think about you. Man, how could you leave me like this? Boy, I was supposed to die before you. I always do things first and come back and tell you and Garvell about it. So what are you doing breaking the cycle? Boy, do I miss you little curly headed man. Big Daddy Buck, man, we did too much together, I love you, man, RIP. Don't you worry, I will be looking out for everybody else as soon as I can get myself together. I will be on Garvell too. So don't worry, little brother, I'm going to put it down just like we always planned. So rest in peace and one love forever. All of my nieces and my nephews and cousins and friends, there are just too many of you to name. I don't want anybody steppin' to me trying to check me so I'm not even going to try and go there. This is going out to all of you and to my LA family, OG Batman, Big Bapa (RIP), my sis Karen (RIP), Big Gee, Linda, Crip Jackie, and all of the Latin King's family and the 6900 Block East Coast family. My little brother Tootie from Compton, my mother-in-law Grace Sanchez (RIP), I love you for always treating me like I'm your flesh-and-blood son. I know I may not have told you that a lot.But it really meant a lot to me. Love ya always and thank you so much for being there for us when we needed you. To my Compton brothers, Raul Brandon and Marcus Lindsay, everything is going to work out. Just remember for every dark day, there are three light days. The sun will shine again. Raul, keep your head up and develop a relationship with God if you haven't already because he really is waiting on you to start talking to him before it's too late. Love ya, I got ya back always no matter what and believe that. To my brother Clifford Sanchez I know, I don't know you like that but ya still my family regardless so peace to you and all of yours, and may God bless you all. To my syndicate family

Ice T and Shaun-E-Shaun peace. My crazy Southern Rap Commission click, you guys are the craziest, but you all are still my family so let's do what we know to do and stay out of trouble okay. The whole gang up at Miramax Films, I love you all. You know who you all are, peace and let's continue to party. The whole click with the Dirty Squirrel, Wild Turkey, the G Spot, and the rest of the gang. Let's keep putting it down. All the homies on lockdown, get it right and come on back home alive, and let's hook things up right, okay!

LaMoney, stay strong dog, and God is the only way, to peace! This book is dedicated to my RIP family: my mother Mary L. Carney; my mother Graciela Sanchez for always keeping it one hundred, love y'all for keeping me real; my baby sister Mary Ellen Jackson, my big brother Clinton Ray Johnson Jr. a.k.a. Butch. One love to my big brother Bruce Carney, Fredrick L. Smith a.k.a. Freaked-out Freddy, my little brother; my beloved niece Anika Layon Scott, my nephew Reggie L Smith, rest in peace; and Samuel E Jackson, my brother-in-law, Big Daddy Buck, Big Poppa East Coast, 69 Crips, my sister Karen Davis, my adopted father, Dr. Joseph Jennings, for keeping me rooted in the Lord Jesus Christ, Ed Slade and Bertha Savoid and many more, with and without names who died dedicated to the street game, rest in peace.

For everyone that died caught up in this crazy street warfare, this book is also dedicated to you. "So rest in peace."

We really need to chill with all of this gang and street madness.

Don't glamorize nothing in this book because if you do, then you are reading and taking it the wrong way. This book is only to educate you from making all the mistakes in life that me and my brothers have made. So please learn from our mistakes and search for Jesus Christ our Lord and our Savior. It is the only way.

I have been to the other side, and I am telling you, you do not want to travel down that road, so try to make it to the light because I want to see you all make it to the other side where the prize really is! Peace and one love. From Gangsta Tea, I'm out!

CPSIA information can be obtained
at www.ICGtesting.com
Printed in the USA
FSOW03n0623130816
23668FS